Jack Nicklaus Does It Again!

First, *The Swing From A–Z...*
Now, *The Short Game and Scoring!*

Stop adding extra strokes...Learn to focus...Increase your self-confidence...Keep on trying!

Golf pro Jack Nicklaus now explains every aspect of the short game by exposing his personal winning tournament tactics!

Here are his fundamentals of good strategy:

- Observe and plan *before* you hit
- "Blank out" the bad shots
- Try to stay relaxed
- Work on your "visualization"
- Think "target" not "trouble"
- Go with your natural "shape"
- Don't fight the inevitable
- Play the percentages
- Beware the easy-looking holes
- Take it easy after a lay-off

Books by Jack Nicklaus (with Ken Bowden)

Play Better Golf: The Swing From A-Z
Play Better Golf, Volume II: The Short Game and Scoring
Play Better Golf, Volume III: Short Cuts to Lower Scores

Published by POCKET BOOKS

Most Pocket Books are available at special quantity discounts for bulk purchases for sales promotions, premiums or fund raising. Special books or book excerpts can also be created to fit specific needs.

For details write the office of the Vice President of Special Markets, Pocket Books, 1230 Avenue of the Americas, New York, New York 10020.

PLAY BETTER GOLF

VOLUME II

THE SHORT GAME AND SCORING

Jack Nicklaus

With Ken Bowden
Illustrated by Jim McQueen

PUBLISHED BY POCKET BOOKS NEW YORK

All drawings contained in this work have been previously
published by King Features, Inc.

Another *Original* publication of POCKET BOOKS

POCKET BOOKS, a division of Simon & Schuster, Inc.
1230 Avenue of the Americas, New York, N.Y. 10020

ISBN: 0-671-63257-4

First Pocket Books printing June, 1981

10 9 8 7 6

POCKET and colophon are registered trademarks
of Simon & Schuster, Inc.

Printed in the U.S.A.

Contents

Introduction

There are two ways to lower your golf score.

The longer and harder way is to improve your full shots: extend your drives, take the bends out of those fairway woods and long irons, sharpen up the medium irons—in effect, build yourself a better swing. This is the longer and harder route because it requires a lot of time, energy, patience and knowledge, not to mention a sound physique and good coordination. However, there's great satisfaction in becoming a better full-shot golfer, and if that's your aim, now or in the future, I'd refer you to the first book in this series, *The Swing from A-Z*.

The shorter and much easier way to lower your golf score is to improve your short game and your strategizing: to tighten up on your technique around and on the greens, plus the way you think and map yourself around the course. This is the easier and quicker route because, once you know the proper techniques, the shorter shots require much less physical strength and dexterity to play well than the big shots, and because the only things you need to do to improve at course management are look and think a little harder before playing your shots.

This book is for those who would like to take the faster and simpler route to lower scores. In the first half I cover all facets of short-game technique, but with particular emphasis on putting because that's almost fifty per cent of the game of golf.

In the book's second half I've tried to present the specific strategies and tactics that have, I believe, been my greatest personal golfing weapons during my twenty years as a professional.

As with *The Swing from A-Z*, all the articles herein were originally created for distribution to newspapers throughout the world by King Features Syndicate of New York, and I again thank my friends at King for their fine efforts in that direction.

Jack Nicklaus

North Palm Beach, Florida, 1981

PLAY BETTER GOLF

Part ONE

Around
the Green

1

From 100 Yards on In

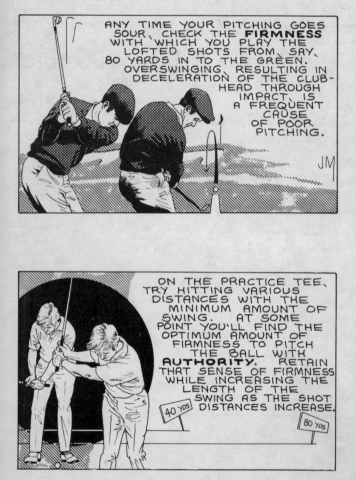

ANY TIME YOUR PITCHING GOES SOUR, CHECK THE **FIRMNESS** WITH WHICH YOU PLAY THE LOFTED SHOTS FROM, SAY, 80 YARDS IN TO THE GREEN. OVERSWINGING, RESULTING IN DECELERATION OF THE CLUB-HEAD THROUGH IMPACT, IS A FREQUENT CAUSE OF POOR PITCHING.

JM

ON THE PRACTICE TEE, TRY HITTING VARIOUS DISTANCES WITH THE MINIMUM AMOUNT OF SWING. AT SOME POINT YOU'LL FIND THE OPTIMUM AMOUNT OF FIRMNESS TO PITCH THE BALL WITH **AUTHORITY**. RETAIN THAT SENSE OF FIRMNESS WHILE INCREASING THE LENGTH OF THE SWING AS THE SHOT DISTANCES INCREASE.

40 YDS

80 YDS

. . . and Stand Firmly

BE FIRM ON YOUR FEET WHEN PLAYING PITCH SHOTS.

FOR MOST REGULAR SHORT SHOTS WITH THE WEDGES, I SET MOST OF MY WEIGHT ON MY LEFT FOOT AND KEEP IT THERE THROUGHOUT THE SWING.

IF YOU SWING SMOOTHLY THERE WILL NATURALLY BE A LITTLE KNEE ACTION AS YOU GO BACK AND THROUGH, BUT THERE'S NO NEED FOR A LOT OF FOOT ACTION. IN FACT, IF YOU WATCH THE TOUR PLAYERS YOU'LL NOTICE THERE IS VERY LITTLE LIFTING OF THE HEELS ON THESE SHORT, HIGH-FLYING SHOTS.

Set Up Open for Greater Control

WHY DO GOOD GOLFERS USUALLY SET UP A LITTLE OPEN — AIMED LEFT OF TARGET IN THEIR FEET AND HIPS — WHEN PITCHING THE BALL?

THERE ARE TWO REASONS.

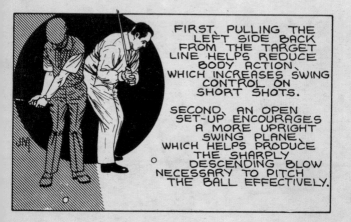

FIRST, PULLING THE LEFT SIDE BACK FROM THE TARGET LINE HELPS REDUCE BODY ACTION, WHICH INCREASES SWING CONTROL ON SHORT SHOTS.

SECOND, AN OPEN SET-UP ENCOURAGES A MORE UPRIGHT SWING PLANE, WHICH HELPS PRODUCE THE SHARPLY DESCENDING BLOW NECESSARY TO PITCH THE BALL EFFECTIVELY.

THE MAIN PURPOSE OF THE WEDGE IS TO PROVIDE HEIGHT AND STOPPING POWER.

PLAYING THE BALL WELL BACK IN THE STANCE WITH THESE CLUBS NEGATES BOTH BY DE-LOFTING THE CLUBFACE — YOU MIGHT AS WELL PLAY A 9-IRON.

JM

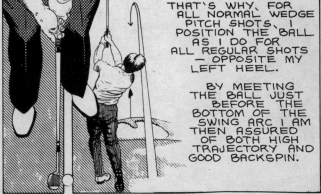

THAT'S WHY, FOR ALL NORMAL WEDGE PITCH SHOTS, I POSITION THE BALL AS I DO FOR ALL REGULAR SHOTS — OPPOSITE MY LEFT HEEL.

BY MEETING THE BALL JUST BEFORE THE BOTTOM OF THE SWING ARC I AM THEN ASSURED OF BOTH HIGH TRAJECTORY AND GOOD BACKSPIN.

Accelerate *the Club Head*

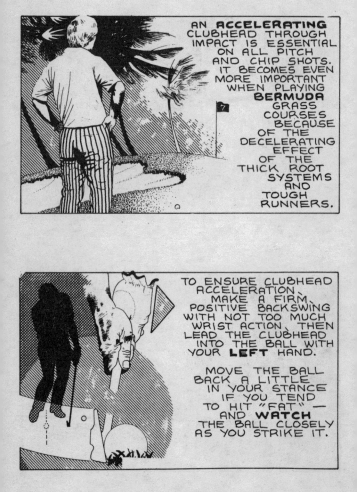

AN **ACCELERATING** CLUBHEAD THROUGH IMPACT IS ESSENTIAL ON ALL PITCH AND CHIP SHOTS. IT BECOMES EVEN MORE IMPORTANT WHEN PLAYING **BERMUDA** GRASS COURSES BECAUSE OF THE DECELERATING EFFECT OF THE THICK ROOT SYSTEMS AND TOUGH RUNNERS.

TO ENSURE CLUBHEAD ACCELERATION, MAKE A FIRM, POSITIVE BACKSWING WITH NOT TOO MUCH WRIST ACTION, THEN LEAD THE CLUBHEAD INTO THE BALL WITH YOUR **LEFT** HAND.

MOVE THE BALL BACK A LITTLE IN YOUR STANCE IF YOU TEND TO HIT "FAT" — AND **WATCH** THE BALL CLOSELY AS YOU STRIKE IT.

Try These Two Methods

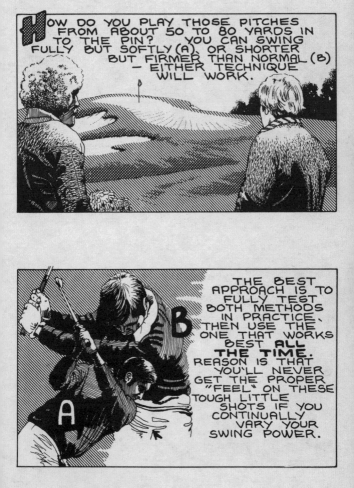

HOW DO YOU PLAY THOSE PITCHES FROM ABOUT 50 TO 80 YARDS IN TO THE PIN? YOU CAN SWING FULLY BUT SOFTLY (A), OR SHORTER BUT FIRMER THAN NORMAL (B) — EITHER TECHNIQUE WILL WORK.

THE BEST APPROACH IS TO FULLY TEST BOTH METHODS IN PRACTICE, THEN USE THE ONE THAT WORKS BEST **ALL THE TIME.** REASON IS THAT YOU'LL NEVER GET THE PROPER "FEEL" ON THESE TOUGH LITTLE SHOTS IF YOU CONTINUALLY VARY YOUR SWING POWER.

Rehearse "Part" Shots Thoroughly

MANY TOUR PLAYERS RARELY TAKE A PRACTICE SWING BEFORE A DRIVE OR OTHER FULL SHOT. BUT YOU'LL NOTICE THAT MOST OF THEM TAKE A NUMBER OF PRACTICE SWINGS BEFORE PLAYING ANY SHOT OF 100 YARDS OR LESS.

WHY?

THE PRACTICE SWINGS ON LESS THAN A FULL SHOT ARE TO 'MEASURE' AND REHEARSE THE LENGTH AND FORCE OF THE STROKE NECESSARY TO HIT THE BALL THE DESIRED DISTANCE.

YOU'LL FIND THE SHORT GAME EASIER IF YOU, TOO, 'FEEL' OUT THE REQUIRED ACTION THOROUGHLY BEFORE STEPPING UP TO THE BALL ON ANYTHING LESS THAN A FULL SHOT.

Don't Neglect the Pitch-and-Run

DON'T OVERLOOK THE PITCH-AND-RUN SHOT WHENEVER HARD GREENS OR HIGH WINDS THREATEN THE HIGH-FLYING PITCH.

PLAY THE SHOT WITH AN EIGHT- OR NINE-IRON, CHOKING WELL DOWN ON THE GRIP AND CONCENTRATING ON MAKING SOLID CONTACT WITH THE BACK OF THE BALL.

ALLOW FOR THE BALL TO RUN ABOUT AS FAR AS IT FLIES IN WINDLESS CONDITIONS, BUT REDUCE OR INCREASE THE ROLL ALLOWANCE FOR HEAD OR TAIL WINDS.

Use Sand-wedge for Extra Height

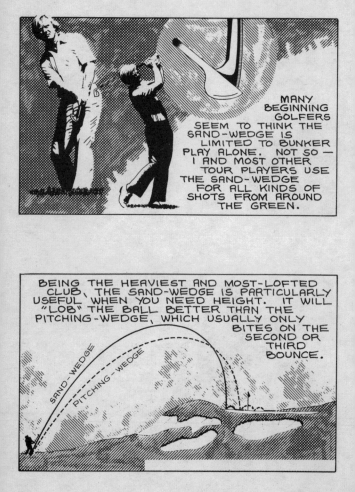

MANY BEGINNING GOLFERS SEEM TO THINK THE SAND-WEDGE IS LIMITED TO BUNKER PLAY ALONE. NOT SO — I AND MOST OTHER TOUR PLAYERS USE THE SAND-WEDGE FOR ALL KINDS OF SHOTS FROM AROUND THE GREEN.

BEING THE HEAVIEST AND MOST-LOFTED CLUB, THE SAND-WEDGE IS PARTICULARLY USEFUL WHEN YOU NEED HEIGHT. IT WILL "LOB" THE BALL BETTER THAN THE PITCHING-WEDGE, WHICH USUALLY ONLY BITES ON THE SECOND OR THIRD BOUNCE.

SAND-WEDGE

PITCHING-WEDGE

Swing Slow and Easy for Short Lob

A SHORT RECOVERY SHOT THAT MUST CLEAR A GREENSIDE OBSTACLE AND STOP QUICKLY REQUIRES A SLOW, EASY SWING WITH VERY FIRM HAND CONTROL. IT NEEDS PRACTICE BECAUSE IT TAKES NERVE, BUT IT'S AN INVALUABLE STROKE-SAVER..ESPECIALLY ON TOUGH COURSES WHERE YOU'RE BOUND TO MISS A NUMBER OF GREENS.

JM

USE A WEDGE, OPEN THE FACE, SWING BACK SLOWLY AND SMOOTHLY WITH THE CLUB FIRMLY GRIPPED IN THE LEFT HAND, THEN MAKE A VERY <u>POSITIVE</u> HIT WITH YOUR **RIGHT** HAND THROUGH IMPACT.

BE SURE NOT TO LET THE LEFT HAND SLACKEN AS THE RIGHT HAND DIRECTS THE BLOW. PROPERLY EXECUTED, THIS SHOT WILL RISE QUICKLY AND SETTLE SOFTLY, EVEN OUT OF FAIRLY HEAVY ROUGH.

Sweep Ball from Uphill Lie

A BALL SITTING CLEANLY ON A GRASSY UPHILL SLOPE NEAR THE GREEN PRESENTS A RELATIVELY EASY SHOT. SIMPLY **SWEEP** THE BALL UP BY LETTING THE CLUB FOLLOW THE SLOPE OF THE GROUND. SWING A LITTLE HARDER TO COMPENSATE FOR A HIGHER TRAJECTORY AND SOFTER LANDING THAN NORMAL.

IF THE BALL IS BURIED IN LONG GRASS, YOU HAVE LITTLE CHOICE BUT TO HIT RIGHT INTO IT AS THOUGH THE LIE WAS LEVEL.

OPEN THE CLUBFACE, KEEP YOUR HEAD VERY STILL, AND TRY TO CATCH THE BALL BEFORE THE CLUB MEETS THE GROUND.

BE **FIRM.**

TOP PRIORITY ON ANY DOWNHILL PITCH SHOT IS TO MEET THE BALL BEFORE THE CLUB CONTACTS THE GROUND — WHICH IS NO EASY TASK IF THE SLOPE IS STEEP.

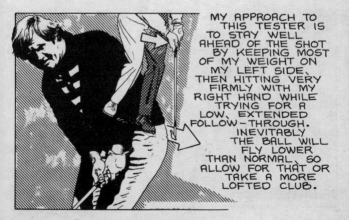

MY APPROACH TO THIS TESTER IS TO STAY WELL AHEAD OF THE SHOT BY KEEPING MOST OF MY WEIGHT ON MY LEFT SIDE, THEN HITTING VERY FIRMLY WITH MY RIGHT HAND WHILE TRYING FOR A LOW, EXTENDED FOLLOW-THROUGH. INEVITABLY THE BALL WILL FLY LOWER THAN NORMAL, SO ALLOW FOR THAT OR TAKE A MORE LOFTED CLUB.

Stand Taller When Ball's Above Feet

FACTOR TO GUARD AGAINST WHEN PITCHING FROM A LIE WHERE THE BALL IS HIGHER THAN YOUR FEET IS CATCHING THE GROUND BEFORE THE CLUB MEETS THE BALL.

COMPENSATE BY STANDING MORE ERECT THAN NORMAL AND POSITIONING THE BALL BACK IN YOUR STANCE WITH YOUR HANDS WELL AHEAD. KEEP YOUR HANDS LEADING THE CLUBFACE THROUGH IMPACT, AND, IF YOU NEED EXTRA HEIGHT, OPEN IT BOTH AT ADDRESS AND AS IT MOVES THROUGH THE BALL.

Keep Clubface Open When Ball's Below Feet

GETTING THE SHOT "UP" AND AVOIDING PUSHING IT RIGHT ARE THE PROBLEMS WHEN CHIPPING OR PITCHING A BALL LYING WELL BELOW YOUR FOOT LEVEL.

ADDRESS THE BALL BACK NEAR YOUR RIGHT FOOT WITH AN OPEN STANCE AND YOUR HANDS WELL AHEAD OF THE CLUBFACE. THEN CUT ACROSS THE BALL BY SWINGING PRONOUNCEDLY FROM OUT TO IN, MAKING SURE YOU DON'T ROLL THE CLUBFACE CLOSED WITH YOUR WRISTS THROUGH IMPACT.

2

From Just Off the Green

Select Club for Maximum Roll

MOST GOLFERS FIND IT EASIER TO JUDGE ROLL THAN FLIGHT, AND IF YOU'RE AMONG THEM THEN SELECTING THE RIGHT CLUB BECOMES THE KEY TO GOOD CHIPPING.

BASIC GOAL IS TO PICK THE CLUB THAT WILL LAND THE BALL A FEW FEET ON THE GREEN AND LET IT ROLL THE REST OF THE WAY TO THE HOLE.

IF YOU WERE SAY 20 YARDS FROM THE PUTTING SURFACE, THIS MIGHT BE AN 8-IRON OR A 9-IRON.

HOWEVER, IF YOU WERE ONLY FOUR OR FIVE YARDS OFF THE GREEN, THEN A LESS LOFTED CLUB WOULD DO THE JOB MORE EASILY — SAY A 5-IRON OR 6-IRON.

"Picture" Shots Mentally

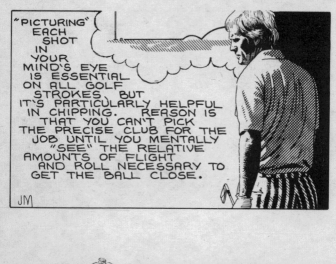

"PICTURING" EACH SHOT IN YOUR MIND'S EYE IS ESSENTIAL ON ALL GOLF STROKES, BUT IT'S PARTICULARLY HELPFUL IN CHIPPING. REASON IS THAT YOU CAN'T PICK THE PRECISE CLUB FOR THE JOB UNTIL YOU MENTALLY "SEE" THE RELATIVE AMOUNTS OF FLIGHT AND ROLL NECESSARY TO GET THE BALL CLOSE.

JM

WHEN PRACTICING CHIPPING I USE VARIOUS CLUBS AND VARIOUS TECHNIQUES, THEN TRY TO COMMIT THE RESULTS TO MEMORY. THIS HELPS GREATLY IN "PICTURING" SHOTS ON THE COURSE ITSELF, NOT LEAST BY REDUCING THE AMOUNT OF GUESSWORK I MUST USE.

Be Deliberate

CHIPPING HAS NEVER COME EASY TO ME, BUT I'VE FOUND OVER THE YEARS THAT THE **SLOWER** MY TEMPO ON THESE LITTLE RECOVERY SHOTS THE BETTER I PLAY THEM.

IT'S ONLY TOO EASY TO JAB OR JERK AT THE BALL WHEN YOU'RE UNDER PRESSURE TO GET IT CLOSE FROM JUST OFF THE GREEN. MY ANTIDOTE TO THAT IS A CONSCIOUS EFFORT TO STROKE <u>DELIBERATELY</u>: TO MAKE AN EASY-YET-FIRM, BUT ABOVE ALL AN **UNHURRIED** SWING.

DELIBERATE

JM

THERE ARE ALMOST AS MANY WAYS TO CHIP AS THERE ARE TO PUTT. BUT MOST GOOD PLAYERS SEEM TO PREFER EITHER AN ALL-WRIST ACTION OR A FAIRLY STIFF-WRISTED ARM STROKE.

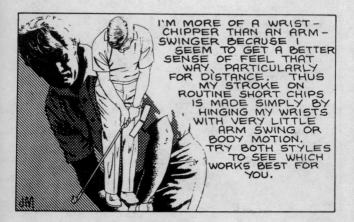

I'M MORE OF A WRIST-CHIPPER THAN AN ARM-SWINGER BECAUSE I SEEM TO GET A BETTER SENSE OF FEEL THAT WAY, PARTICULARLY FOR DISTANCE. THUS MY STROKE ON ROUTINE SHORT CHIPS IS MADE SIMPLY BY HINGING MY WRISTS WITH VERY LITTLE ARM SWING OR BODY MOTION. TRY BOTH STYLES TO SEE WHICH WORKS BEST FOR YOU.

SOME GOLFERS SEEM TO THINK THEY SHOULD GRIP TIGHTER ON A CHIP SHOT, WHILE OTHERS FEEL A LOOSER-THAN-NORMAL GRIP WILL WORK BETTER. BOTH ARE WRONG.

CRISPNESS OF STRIKE IS ESSENTIAL ON CHIP SHOTS, AND YOU WON'T ACHIEVE IT EITHER WITH THE CHOPPY SWING THAT COMES FROM AN OVER-TIGHT GRIP OR THE FLOPPY MOTION THAT COMES FROM A SLOPPY HOLD ON THE CLUB. WHAT <u>WILL</u> ACHIEVE IT IS THE SAME DEGREE OF <u>FIRMNESS</u> IN THE HANDS THAT YOU USE FOR FULL SHOTS.

Choke Down for Better "Touch"

DON'T MAKE THE COMMON MISTAKE OF ROUTINELY HOLDING AS HIGH ON THE CLUB AS YOU DO FOR FULL SHOTS WHEN CHIPPING AND PITCHING.

THE CLOSER YOUR HANDS ARE TO THE CLUBHEAD, THE GREATER YOUR CONTROL AND THE MORE DELICATE YOUR TOUCH. SO LEARN TO CHOKE DOWN ON THE LITTLE SHOTS — USING LESS SHAFT THE MORE GENTLY YOU MUST STROKE AND/OR THE LESS DISTANCE THE BALL MUST TRAVEL.

JM

IF YOUR CHIPPING IS LESS THAN YOU'D LIKE IT TO BE, CONSIDER YOUR DISTANCE FROM THE BALL.

THE FARTHER AWAY YOU STAND, THE MORE THE CLUBHEAD MUST SWING OFF THE TARGET LINE ON BOTH SIDES OF THE BALL, AND THUS THE MORE ITS FACE MUST OPEN AND CLOSE.

STANDING AS CLOSE AS IS COMFORTABLY POSSIBLE FACILITATES A MORE DIRECTLY BACK—AND THROUGH-SWING PATH, AND THUS A BETTER CHANCE OF MEETING THE BALL WITH THE CLUBFACE SQUARE TO THE TARGET LINE.

Swing Through, Not At, Ball

A QUICK AND JERKY CHIPPING STROKE CAN CAUSE YOU A LOT OF PAIN AT GOLF. SO, TOO, CAN AN OVER-DELIBERATE STROKING MOTION, BY CAUSING YOU TO DECELERATE THE CLUBHEAD THROUGH THE BALL.

SMOOTHNESS OF STROKE IS THE QUALITY TO STRIVE FOR.

YOU'LL ACHIEVE THIS MORE EASILY IF YOU PRACTICE SWINGING THE CLUBHEAD **THROUGH**, NOT **AT**, THE BALL.

SUCH A MOTION WILL ALSO PRODUCE ACCELERATION THROUGH THE BALL — A FUNDAMENTAL OF GOOD CHIPPING.

Don't Roll Right Over Left

A LOT OF CHIP SHOTS ARE PULLED LEFT OF TARGET BECAUSE THE RIGHT HAND ROLLS OVER THE LEFT THROUGH IMPACT, CLOSING THE CLUBFACE.

THE FAULT ALSO CAUSES THE BALL TO FLY TOO LOW AND ROLL TOO FAR.

IF YOU'RE PULLING ANY OF THE LITTLE SHOTS, CHECK YOUR HAND ACTION THROUGH IMPACT.

THE FEELING TO STRIVE FOR IS OF THE RIGHT HAND MOVING **UNDER**, NOT OVER, AS IT HITS AGAINST A FIRM, GUIDING LEFT HAND.

JM

Hold Extra Firmly from Rough

IN CHIPPING FROM ROUGH, MAKE SURE YOU HOLD THE CLUB FIRMLY THROUGHOUT THE STROKE TO MINIMIZE THE CHANCE OF THE BLADE BEING TWISTED BY THE LONG GRASS. AND MAKE THE STROKE FIRM, TOO — SLOW, SMOOTH AND DELIBERATE.

I FIND FIRMING UP EVEN MORE WITH MY RIGHT HAND JUST BEFORE IMPACT HELPS ME KEEP THE CLUBFACE SQUARE AND ACCELERATING ON THESE TRICKY LITTLE SHOTS.

BUT PRACTICE THIS TECHNIQUE A WHILE BEFORE YOU TAKE IT ONTO THE COURSE.

Putt from Off Green When Possible

I'LL "TEXAS WEDGE" A SHOT FROM JUST OFF THE GREEN — PUTT THE BALL INSTEAD OF CHIPPING OR PITCHING IT — ANY TIME CONDITIONS ALLOW. THESE ARE GENERALLY IDEAL WHEN THE TURF IS FIRM AND DRY AND FAIRLY EVEN.

TO PLAY THIS SHOT, USE YOUR NORMAL PUTTING TECHNIQUE BUT HIT A LITTLE HARDER THAN YOU NORMALLY WOULD. AND **KEEP YOUR HEAD AND BODY STILL** — THERE'S A GREAT TEMPTATION ON THIS KIND OF STROKE TO "PEEK" TOO EARLY. YOU'LL FIND THIS SHOT PARTICULARLY VALUABLE FROM A THIN LIE.

3

From the Sand

Get Out at First Attempt

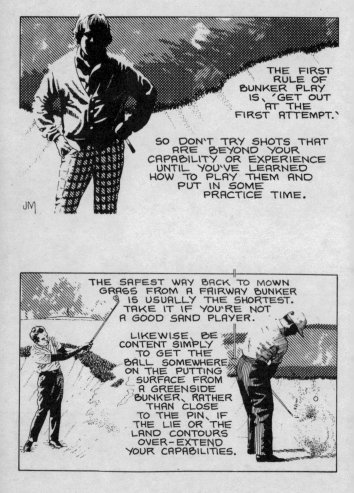

THE FIRST RULE OF BUNKER PLAY IS, 'GET OUT AT THE FIRST ATTEMPT.'

SO DON'T TRY SHOTS THAT ARE BEYOND YOUR CAPABILITY OR EXPERIENCE UNTIL YOU'VE LEARNED HOW TO PLAY THEM AND PUT IN SOME PRACTICE TIME.

JM

THE SAFEST WAY BACK TO MOWN GRASS FROM A FAIRWAY BUNKER IS USUALLY THE SHORTEST. TAKE IT IF YOU'RE NOT A GOOD SAND PLAYER.

LIKEWISE, BE CONTENT SIMPLY TO GET THE BALL SOMEWHERE ON THE PUTTING SURFACE FROM A GREENSIDE BUNKER, RATHER THAN CLOSE TO THE PIN, IF THE LIE OR THE LAND CONTOURS OVER-EXTEND YOUR CAPABILITIES.

Use the Proper Sand Club

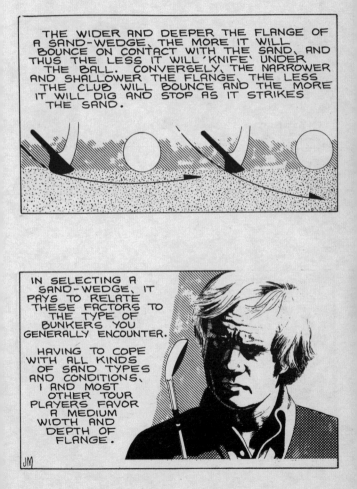

THE WIDER AND DEEPER THE FLANGE OF A SAND-WEDGE, THE MORE IT WILL BOUNCE ON CONTACT WITH THE SAND, AND THUS THE LESS IT WILL 'KNIFE' UNDER THE BALL. CONVERSELY, THE NARROWER AND SHALLOWER THE FLANGE, THE LESS THE CLUB WILL BOUNCE AND THE MORE IT WILL DIG AND STOP AS IT STRIKES THE SAND.

IN SELECTING A SAND-WEDGE, IT PAYS TO RELATE THESE FACTORS TO THE TYPE OF BUNKERS YOU GENERALLY ENCOUNTER.

HAVING TO COPE WITH ALL KINDS OF SAND TYPES AND CONDITIONS, I AND MOST OTHER TOUR PLAYERS FAVOR A MEDIUM WIDTH AND DEPTH OF FLANGE.

JM

Learn to Hit Sand, Not Ball

A LOT OF THE MISSED BUNKER SHOTS I SEE IN PRO-AMS ARE THE RESULT OF TRYING TO "PICK" THE BALL, WHICH IN TURN RESULTS FROM A FEAR OF HITTING SAND INSTEAD OF BALL.

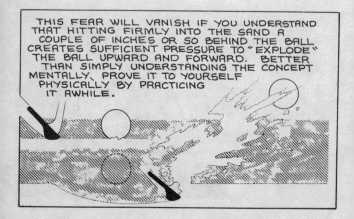

THIS FEAR WILL VANISH IF YOU UNDERSTAND THAT HITTING FIRMLY INTO THE SAND A COUPLE OF INCHES OR SO BEHIND THE BALL CREATES SUFFICIENT PRESSURE TO "EXPLODE" THE BALL UPWARD AND FORWARD. BETTER THAN SIMPLY UNDERSTANDING THE CONCEPT MENTALLY, PROVE IT TO YOURSELF PHYSICALLY BY PRACTICING IT AWHILE.

Think and Swing in Slow Motion

BECAUSE THEY FEAR SAND SHOTS SO DEEPLY, MOST GOLFERS RUSH BOTH THEIR PREPARATION AND THE SWING ITSELF IN AN EFFORT TO GET THE EXPERIENCE OVER AND DONE WITH.

IT'S FREQUENTLY A VERY COSTLY MISTAKE.

APPROACH A BUNKER SHOT BOTH MENTALLY AND PHYSICALLY AS THOUGH YOU WERE THINKING AND PLAYING IN **SLOW MOTION**. REMEMBER, YOU RARELY NEED FORCE TO REMOVE THE BALL A SHORT DISTANCE FROM SAND — JUST REASONABLY ACCURATE CLUB-HEAD DELIVERY.

SO STAY CALM AND KEEP THE TEMPO SLOW, LOOSE AND EASY.

Read Green Slopes Carefully

PLAYED CORRECTLY, ALL NORMAL GREENSIDE BUNKER SHOTS ARE STRUCK WITH A CUTTING OR SLICING ACTION, CAUSING THE BALL TO BREAK TO YOUR RIGHT UPON LANDING.

CAREFUL READING OF GREEN SLOPES IS THUS A KEY ELEMENT IN SUCH SHOTS.

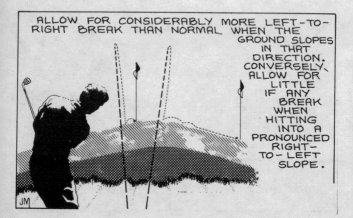

ALLOW FOR CONSIDERABLY MORE LEFT-TO-RIGHT BREAK THAN NORMAL WHEN THE GROUND SLOPES IN THAT DIRECTION. CONVERSELY, ALLOW FOR LITTLE IF ANY BREAK WHEN HITTING INTO A PRONOUNCED RIGHT-TO-LEFT SLOPE.

Keep Clubface Open

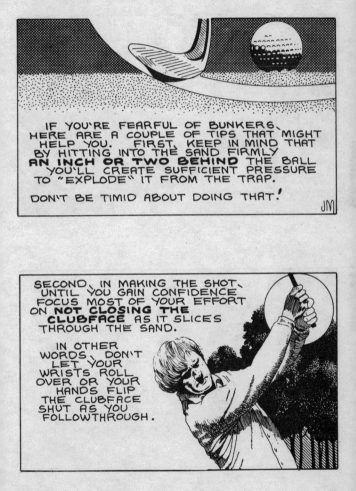

IF YOU'RE FEARFUL OF BUNKERS, HERE ARE A COUPLE OF TIPS THAT MIGHT HELP YOU. FIRST, KEEP IN MIND THAT BY HITTING INTO THE SAND FIRMLY **AN INCH OR TWO BEHIND** THE BALL YOU'LL CREATE SUFFICIENT PRESSURE TO "EXPLODE" IT FROM THE TRAP.

DON'T BE TIMID ABOUT DOING THAT!

JM

SECOND, IN MAKING THE SHOT, UNTIL YOU GAIN CONFIDENCE FOCUS MOST OF YOUR EFFORT ON **NOT CLOSING THE CLUBFACE** AS IT SLICES THROUGH THE SAND.

IN OTHER WORDS, DON'T LET YOUR WRISTS ROLL OVER OR YOUR HANDS FLIP THE CLUBFACE SHUT AS YOU FOLLOWTHROUGH.

A BASIC OF BUNKER PLAY, APPLICABLE TO EVERY TYPE OF SHOT, IS TO ESTABLISH A FIRM STANCE BY DIGGING AND SHUFFLING YOUR FEET WELL INTO THE SAND.

IN DOING THAT, BE SURE THAT YOU ALSO <u>CHOKE DOWN</u> ON THE CLUB TO ADJUST FOR HAVING PUT YOUR HANDS <u>CLOSER</u> TO THE BALL.

MANY GOLFERS WHO HIT TOO DEEPLY INTO THE SAND DO SO AS A RESULT OF FORGETTING TO MAKE THIS COMPENSATION.

Test Sand Texture with Feet

TESTING THE TEXTURE OF BUNKER SAND WITH YOUR HANDS OR THE CLUB IS ILLEGAL, BUT THE RULES DO ALLOW WIGGLING THE FEET AROUND AS MUCH AS YOU LIKE.

SO, WHILE THEY'RE BUILDING YOU A NICE FIRM STANCE, USE THEM ALSO TO TRANSMIT INFORMATION ABOUT THE SAND TEXTURE.

A GOOD 'RULE OF FOOT' IS THAT THE SOFTER THE SUBSURFACE OF THE SAND, THE LESS THE CLUB WILL BOUNCE OR KNIFE THROUGH IT, THUS THE HARDER YOU MUST SWING.

AND, OF COURSE, VICE VERSA IN FIRM SAND.

Decide Your Preferred Method

TO VARY DISTANCE ON "EXPLOSION"-TYPE SHOTS FROM SAND, YOU CAN VARY EITHER THE FORCE OF THE SWING OR THE DEPTH OF THE CUT YOU TAKE — OR A COMBINATION OF BOTH.

TOUR PLAYERS USE ALL THREE TECHNIQUES.

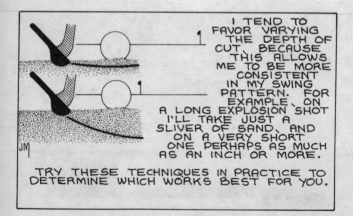

I TEND TO FAVOR VARYING THE DEPTH OF CUT, BECAUSE THIS ALLOWS ME TO BE MORE CONSISTENT IN MY SWING PATTERN. FOR EXAMPLE, ON A LONG EXPLOSION SHOT I'LL TAKE JUST A SLIVER OF SAND, AND ON A VERY SHORT ONE PERHAPS AS MUCH AS AN INCH OR MORE.

TRY THESE TECHNIQUES IN PRACTICE TO DETERMINE WHICH WORKS BEST FOR YOU.

Picture Removing Area of Sand

HERE'S A SAND-
SHOT TIP THAT
HELPED ME TREMENDOUSLY SOME YEARS
AGO, AND THAT COULD DO THE SAME
FOR YOU. INSTEAD OF THINKING OF
HITTING AT A CERTAIN POINT BEHIND
THE BALL, CONCENTRATE INSTEAD ON
AN **AREA** OF SAND.

ENVISION A RECTANGLE ABOUT
SIX INCHES LONG AND THREE
INCHES WIDE OF WHICH THE
BALL IS PART. REMOVE THIS
AREA FROM THE BUNKER AND
YOU'LL ALSO REMOVE THE BALL.

CUT OUT A SHALLOWER
SLAB THE FARTHER YOU
WANT THE BALL TO GO,
OR TAKE THE SAME
CUT AND HIT HARDER.

Vary Depth of Cut
for Special Effects

VARYING THE <u>DEPTH</u> YOU HIT UNDER THE BALL PRODUCES VARYING EFFECTS FROM SAND. FOR EXAMPLE, HIT <u>SHALLOW</u> AND WELL <u>BEHIND</u> THE BALL AND YOU'LL PRODUCE A SOFT SHOT WITH LITTLE BACKSPIN.

HIT <u>DEEP</u> AND FAR BEHIND THE BALL (AS FOR A BURIED LIE) AND THE BALL WILL RUN ON LANDING. HIT <u>SHALLOW</u> AND <u>CLOSE</u> AND THE HEAVY BACKSPIN IMPARTED WILL STOP THE BALL QUICKLY.

OCCASIONALLY PRACTICING THESE DIFFERENT TECHNIQUES WILL VASTLY IMPROVE YOUR "RECOVERY" GAME.

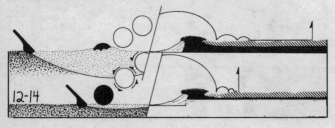

12-14

Relate Swing Force to Chipping

IF YOUR BUNKER-SHOT TECHNIQUE IS TO VARY DISTANCES BY THE FORCE OF THE SWING, HERE'S A MEANS OF GUAGING HOW MUCH POWER IS REQUIRED THAT HAS HELPED ME OVER THE YEARS.

JM

SIMPLY PROGRAM YOURSELF TO SWING AS HARD FROM SAND AS YOU WOULD FOR A CHIP SHOT FROM DOUBLE THE DISTANCE.

FOR INSTANCE, IF YOU HAVE A 30-FOOT SAND SHOT, THINK OF THE FORCE NEEDED FOR A 60-FOOT CHIP SHOT, AND SO ON.

0314

30'

60'

Hit Steeply under Buried Lie

GETTING THE BALL CLOSE TO THE PIN FROM A BURIED LIE WHEN YOU HAVE VERY LITTLE GREEN TO WORK WITH IS ONE OF THE TOUGHEST SHOTS IN GOLF — SOMETIMES TO THE POINT OF BEING IMPOSSIBLE.

MY TECHNIQUE ON THIS SHOT STARTS WITH A WIDE-OPEN CLUBFACE AT ADDRESS, PLUS A QUICK WRIST-BREAK GOING BACK TO CREATE A VERY STEEP ANGLE OF ATTACK COMING DOWN. THEN I CONCENTRATE ON GETTING WELL UNDER THE BALL BY DRIVING THE CLUBHEAD DEEP INTO THE SAND ABOUT AN INCH BEHIND IT, HITTING VERY FORCEFULLY WITH MY RIGHT HAND.

Swing "Low" to Beat Wet Sand

WET COMPACTED SAND IS OFTEN EASIER TO PLAY FROM THAN DRY, POWDERY SAND, SO LONG AS YOU KNOW HOW. START BY POSITIONING THE BALL OPPOSITE YOUR LEFT HEEL AND SET THE SAND-WEDGE FACE WIDE OPEN.

THEN MAKE A SHORT, **OUTSIDE** AND **LOW** BACKSWING, HITTING ABOUT AN INCH BEHIND THE BALL.

THE CUSHIONING EFFECT OF THE SAND, PLUS THE LOW BACKSWING AND OPEN FACE, WILL KEEP THE CLUB FROM DIGGING TOO DEEPLY.

Adjust Posture When Ball's Below . . .

KEY TO **THIS** SHOT IS ADJUSTING YOUR BODY SO YOU CAN SWING PRETTY MUCH AS YOU WOULD FROM A LEVEL LIE.

GRIP THE CLUB CLOSE TO ITS END, THEN BEND YOUR KNEES AS FAR AS NECESSARY TO GET FULLY **DOWN** TO THE BALL.

AIM MORE TO THE LEFT THAN USUAL TO ALLOW FOR THE BALL'S TENDENCY TO FLY RIGHT, THEN SWING AS FOR A NORMAL SAND SHOT.

ABOVE ALL, KEEP YOUR <u>HEAD STILL</u> UNTIL WELL AFTER IMPACT.

AS WHEN THE BALL IS BELOW YOUR FEET, THE WAY YOU SET UP IS THE KEY TO THIS FREQUENTLY-ENCOUNTERED SAND SHOT.

'DISTANCE' YOURSELF CORRECTLY FROM THE BALL BY CHOKING DOWN ON THE CLUB AND STANDING MORE ERECT THAN NORMAL. AIM RIGHT TO ALLOW FOR THE BALL'S TENDENCY TO FLY LEFT, THEN SWING AS YOU USUALLY DO ON A BUNKER SHOT. BE SURE NOT TO LET THE CLUBFACE CLOSE AS YOU HIT THROUGH THE SAND.

57

Don't Give Up on This One

DON'T GIVE UP ON THE SHOT PICTURED HERE, BECAUSE GETTING IT WITHIN AT LEAST TWO-PUTT DISTANCE IS
(A) NOT IMPOSSIBLE, AND
(B) WILL GIVE YOU A NICE PSYCHOLOGICAL BOOST.

TAKE A SOLID STANCE, CHOKE DOWN ON THE CLUB, OPEN THE FACE WIDE, COCK YOUR WRISTS SHARPLY WHILE SWINGING BACK TO THE OUTSIDE, THEN HIT INTO THE SAND VERY FIRMLY WITH YOUR RIGHT HAND AS CLOSE TO THE BALL AS POSSIBLE.

Consider a Chip Shot

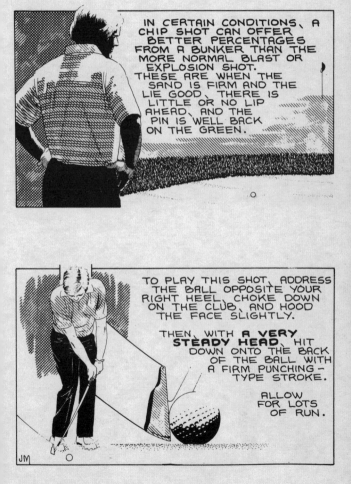

IN CERTAIN CONDITIONS, A CHIP SHOT CAN OFFER BETTER PERCENTAGES FROM A BUNKER THAN THE MORE NORMAL BLAST OR EXPLOSION SHOT.
THESE ARE WHEN THE SAND IS FIRM AND THE LIE GOOD, THERE IS LITTLE OR NO LIP AHEAD, AND THE PIN IS WELL BACK ON THE GREEN.

TO PLAY THIS SHOT, ADDRESS THE BALL OPPOSITE YOUR RIGHT HEEL, CHOKE DOWN ON THE CLUB, AND HOOD THE FACE SLIGHTLY.

THEN, WITH **A VERY STEADY HEAD**, HIT DOWN ONTO THE BACK OF THE BALL WITH A FIRM PUNCHING-TYPE STROKE.

ALLOW FOR LOTS OF RUN.

JM

Putt Ball When Conditions Allow

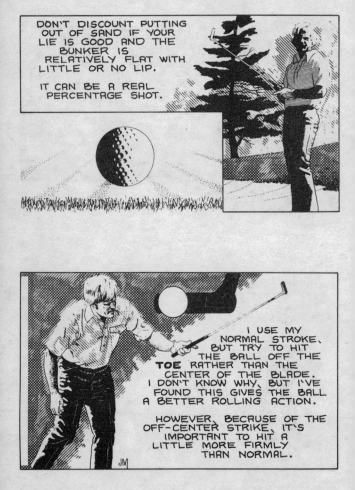

DON'T DISCOUNT PUTTING OUT OF SAND IF YOUR LIE IS GOOD AND THE BUNKER IS RELATIVELY FLAT WITH LITTLE OR NO LIP.

IT CAN BE A REAL PERCENTAGE SHOT.

I USE MY NORMAL STROKE, BUT TRY TO HIT THE BALL OFF THE **TOE** RATHER THAN THE CENTER OF THE BLADE. I DON'T KNOW WHY, BUT I'VE FOUND THIS GIVES THE BALL A BETTER ROLLING ACTION.

HOWEVER, BECAUSE OF THE OFF-CENTER STRIKE, IT'S IMPORTANT TO HIT A LITTLE MORE FIRMLY THAN NORMAL.

JM

Swallow Pride—and Play Safe

MIRACLES RARELY HAPPEN AT GOLF, AND ALMOST NEVER FROM BUNKERS. SO DON'T BE FOOLHARDY IN A SITUATION LIKE THIS. TAKE YOUR PUNISHMENT AND TAKE THE **SAFE** WAY ONTO THE GREEN.

PLAYING AWAY FROM THE HOLE WILL CERTAINLY GIVE YOU A LONGER PUTT THAN YOU'D LIKE.

BUT, NO MATTER HOW LONG IT IS, IT'S BETTER THAN FACING THE SAME SHOT OVER AGAIN... AND AGAIN... AND AGAIN...

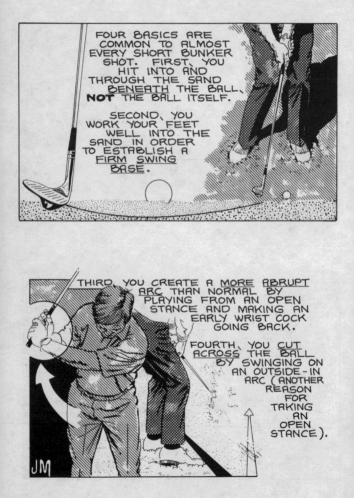

FOUR BASICS ARE COMMON TO ALMOST EVERY SHORT BUNKER SHOT. FIRST, YOU HIT INTO AND THROUGH THE SAND <u>BENEATH THE BALL</u>, **NOT** THE BALL ITSELF.

SECOND, YOU WORK YOUR FEET WELL INTO THE SAND IN ORDER TO ESTABLISH A <u>FIRM SWING BASE</u>.

THIRD, YOU CREATE A <u>MORE ABRUPT ARC</u> THAN NORMAL BY PLAYING FROM AN OPEN STANCE AND MAKING AN EARLY WRIST COCK GOING BACK.

FOURTH, YOU <u>CUT ACROSS</u> THE BALL BY SWINGING ON AN OUTSIDE-IN ARC (ANOTHER REASON FOR TAKING AN OPEN STANCE).

JM

Part **TWO**

On the
Green

4

Six Principles for Good Putting

Find Style That Works Best for You

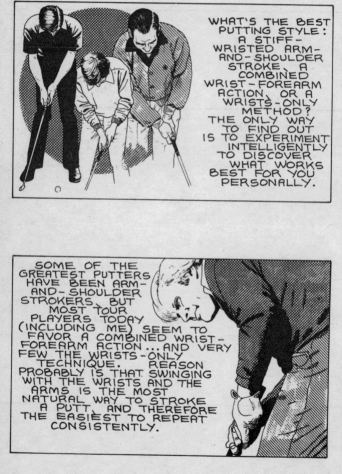

WHAT'S THE BEST PUTTING STYLE: A STIFF-WRISTED ARM-AND-SHOULDER STROKE, A COMBINED WRIST-FOREARM ACTION, OR A WRISTS-ONLY METHOD? THE ONLY WAY TO FIND OUT IS TO EXPERIMENT INTELLIGENTLY TO DISCOVER WHAT WORKS BEST FOR YOU PERSONALLY.

SOME OF THE GREATEST PUTTERS HAVE BEEN ARM-AND-SHOULDER STROKERS, BUT MOST TOUR PLAYERS TODAY (INCLUDING ME) SEEM TO FAVOR A COMBINED WRIST-FOREARM ACTION... AND VERY FEW THE WRISTS-ONLY TECHNIQUE. REASON PROBABLY IS THAT SWINGING WITH THE WRISTS AND THE ARMS IS THE MOST NATURAL WAY TO STROKE A PUTT, AND THEREFORE THE EASIEST TO REPEAT CONSISTENTLY.

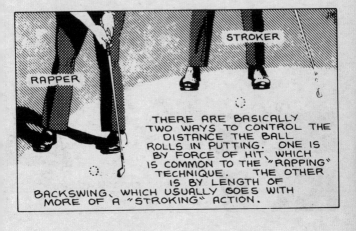

RAPPER

STROKER

THERE ARE BASICALLY TWO WAYS TO CONTROL THE DISTANCE THE BALL ROLLS IN PUTTING. ONE IS BY FORCE OF HIT, WHICH IS COMMON TO THE "RAPPING" TECHNIQUE. THE OTHER IS BY LENGTH OF BACKSWING, WHICH USUALLY GOES WITH MORE OF A "STROKING" ACTION.

I'M PRINCIPALLY A STROKER. AS PUTTS LENGTHEN, SO OBVIOUSLY THE FORCE YOU APPLY IS BOUND TO INCREASE. HOWEVER, I GOVERN DISTANCE CHIEFLY BY VARYING THE LENGTH OF MY BACKSWING, TRYING TO SUSTAIN A CONSTANT PACE AND STRENGTH OF STROKE ON ALL PUTTS.

SHORT PUTT

LONGER PUTT

Be Consistent in Your Method

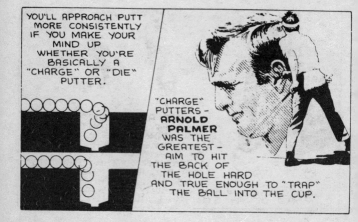

YOU'LL APPROACH PUTT MORE CONSISTENTLY IF YOU MAKE YOUR MIND UP WHETHER YOU'RE BASICALLY A "CHARGE" OR "DIE" PUTTER.

"CHARGE" PUTTERS - **ARNOLD PALMER** WAS THE GREATEST - AIM TO HIT THE BACK OF THE HOLE HARD AND TRUE ENOUGH TO "TRAP" THE BALL INTO THE CUP.

I'M A <u>DIE</u> PUTTER BECAUSE I THINK IT OFFERS BETTER PERCENTAGES.

I AIM TO DROP THE BALL JUST OVER THE FRONT EDGE OF THE CUP WHEN I STROKE IT PERFECTLY, OR TOPPLE IT IN THE SIDES WHEN I DON'T.

Find and Stick to Ideal Putter

I'VE CHANGED PUTTERS ON ONLY TWO OR THREE OCCASIONS DURING MY CAREER, BECAUSE I BELIEVE IT'S THE "PUTTEE," NOT THE PUTTER, THAT DETERMINES WHAT WILL HAPPEN TO THE BALL.

SO MY ADVICE IS TO FIND A PUTTER YOU LIKE — THAT GIVES YOU THE BEST **FEEL** DAY IN, DAY OUT — AND STICK TO IT.
ONE FACTOR TO WATCH FOR IN SELECTING A PUTTER IS WEIGHT: IF YOUR GREENS ARE NORMALLY FAST, THEN YOU'LL PROBABLY DO BEST WITH A LIGHT PUTTER, AND THE REVERSE IF THEY ARE GENERALLY SLOW.

Look for Good Balance, Proper Lie

FINDING A WEIGHT AND BALANCE OF CLUB THAT FEELS GOOD IS A BIG FACTOR IN SELECTING A PUTTER.

AN EQUALLY IMPORTANT POINT IS HOW THE HEAD SITS WHEN YOU ASSUME YOUR MOST EFFECTIVE PUTTING STANCE.

JM

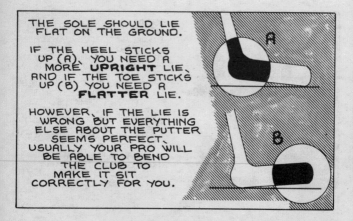

THE SOLE SHOULD LIE FLAT ON THE GROUND.

IF THE HEEL STICKS UP (A), YOU NEED A MORE **UPRIGHT** LIE, AND IF THE TOE STICKS UP (B) YOU NEED A **FLATTER** LIE.

HOWEVER, IF THE LIE IS WRONG BUT EVERYTHING ELSE ABOUT THE PUTTER SEEMS PERFECT, USUALLY YOUR PRO WILL BE ABLE TO BEND THE CLUB TO MAKE IT SIT CORRECTLY FOR YOU.

A

B

Build Confidence in Your Stroke

DON'T GET INTO THE HABIT OF DISCOUNTING OR DISLIKING PUTTING AS A PART OF THE GAME OF GOLF.

REMEMBER, YOU MAY BE ABLE TO RECOVER FROM A MISSED DRIVE OR APPROACH, BUT A MISSED PUTT IS A STROKE GONE FOREVER.

ABSOLUTE ESSENTIAL FOR GOOD PUTTING IS A SOUND METHOD OF STROKING THE BALL. IF YOU LACK CONFIDENCE IN **HOW** YOU'RE GOING TO HIT A PUTT, YOU'LL HAVE EVEN LESS ABOUT **WHERE** YOU'RE GOING TO HIT IT. SO WORK ON THAT STROKE EVERY CHANCE YOU GET!

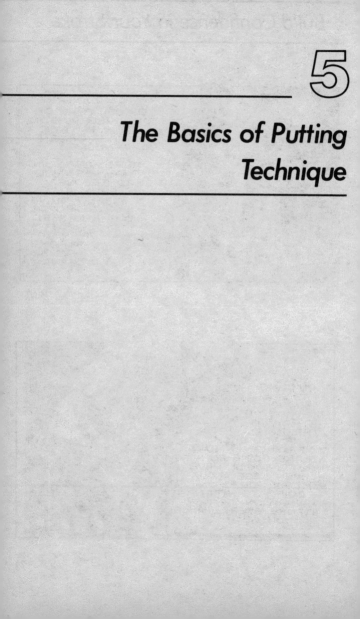

5

The Basics of Putting Technique

Six Factors for Good Putting

WHAT MAKES A GOOD PUTTER?

HERE ARE SOME OF THE PHYSICAL FACTORS THAT I HAVE NOTED OVER THE YEARS.
1. VERY STILL HEAD AND BODY.
2. SMOOTHNESS OF STROKE, EVENNESS OF TEMPO.
3. PUTTERHEAD ACCELERATES THROUGH BALL.

AND ON THE MENTAL SIDE:
1. A GENERALLY POSITIVE ATTITUDE TO THIS CRITICAL PART OF THE GAME.
2. CARE, PRECISION AND SKILL IN READING ALL TYPES OF GREENS.
3. CONFIDENCE.

JM

Grip to Stroke Ball Squarely

HOW SHOULD YOU HOLD A PUTTER?

THE ANSWER IS WHICHEVER WAY BEST ENABLES YOU TO SWING THE PUTTER BLADE THROUGH THE BALL SQUARE TO ITS INTENDED STARTING LINE.

MOST PEOPLE FIND THIS HAPPENS WHEN THEIR PALMS ARE SQUARELY ALIGNED WITH THE PUTTER BLADE. IN MY CASE, IT'S PARTICULARLY IMPORTANT TO HAVE THE **RIGHT** HAND FACING THUS, SO I CAN IN EFFECT USE IT TO "PUSH" THE PUTTER HEAD THROUGH THE BALL DIRECTLY ALONG ITS STARTING LINE.

Work for a Fluid Motion

HOW TIGHTLY SHOULD YOU HOLD YOUR PUTTER?

TO ME, THE MOST IMPORTANT CONSIDERATION IN PUTTING IS **FLUIDITY** OF STROKE, AND GRIP FIRMNESS HAS A BIG INFLUENCE ON THAT.

I TRY TO HOLD THE PUTTER SUFFICIENTLY FIRMLY TO BE ABLE TO CONTROL ITS PATH AND FACE ALIGNMENT, BUT NOT SO FIRMLY THAT IT CAN'T SWING NATURALLY OF ITS OWN WEIGHT. YOU MIGHT FIND IT WORTH SOME EXPERIMENTATION TO DISCOVER EXACTLY WHAT "WEIGHT" OF GRIP ALLOWS YOU TO MEET THOSE STROKING IDEALS.

Guide with Left, Hit with Right

WHICH IS THE MASTER HAND IN PUTTING?

AS WITH SO MANY GOLFING QUESTIONS THE ANSWER HAS TO BE "THAT DEPENDS...

SOME GREAT PUTTERS HAVE FELT THE LEFT HAND TO BE IN COMMAND. OTHERS HAVE SWORN THAT THE RIGHT WAS THE KEY.

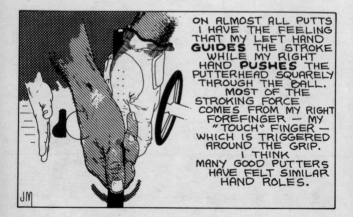

ON ALMOST ALL PUTTS I HAVE THE FEELING THAT MY LEFT HAND **GUIDES** THE STROKE WHILE MY RIGHT HAND **PUSHES** THE PUTTERHEAD SQUARELY THROUGH THE BALL. MOST OF THE STROKING FORCE COMES FROM MY RIGHT FOREFINGER — MY "TOUCH" FINGER — WHICH IS TRIGGERED AROUND THE GRIP. I THINK MANY GOOD PUTTERS HAVE FELT SIMILAR HAND ROLES.

JM

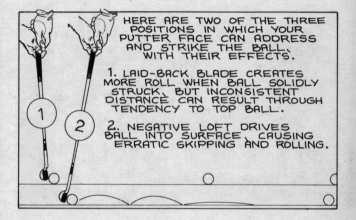

HERE ARE TWO OF THE THREE POSITIONS IN WHICH YOUR PUTTER FACE CAN ADDRESS AND STRIKE THE BALL, WITH THEIR EFFECTS.

1. LAID-BACK BLADE CREATES MORE ROLL WHEN BALL SOLIDLY STRUCK, BUT INCONSISTENT DISTANCE CAN RESULT THROUGH TENDENCY TO TOP BALL.

2. NEGATIVE LOFT DRIVES BALL INTO SURFACE, CAUSING ERRATIC SKIPPING AND ROLLING.

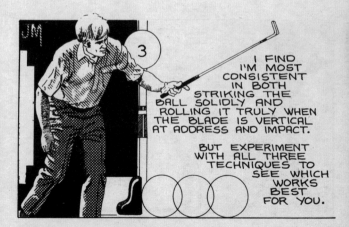

I FIND I'M MOST CONSISTENT IN BOTH STRIKING THE BALL SOLIDLY AND ROLLING IT TRULY WHEN THE BLADE IS VERTICAL AT ADDRESS AND IMPACT.

BUT EXPERIMENT WITH ALL THREE TECHNIQUES TO SEE WHICH WORKS BEST FOR YOU.

Meet These Two Set-Up Goals

WHAT'S THE PROPER STANCE AND POSTURE FOR PUTTING?

FRANKLY, I DON'T THINK SUCH THINGS EXIST. WATCH THE **PGA** TOUR AND YOU'LL SEE JUST ABOUT AS MANY VARIATIONS AS THERE ARE PLAYERS.

ALL, HOWEVER, TRY TO MEET AT LEAST TWO GOALS.

NUMBER ONE IS GOOD BALANCE — A FEELING OF COMFORT AND STABILITY. NUMBER TWO IS A SET-UP THAT POSITIONS THE EYES DIRECTLY OVER THE BALL AND ALLOWS THE HEAD TO REMAIN VERY STILL THROUGHOUT THE STROKE — "MUSTS" FOR GOOD STROKING.

Set Weight to Stabilize Body

HOW SHOULD YOUR WEIGHT BE DISTRIBUTED WHEN PUTTING?

WHICHEVER WAY BEST ALLOWS YOU TO KEEP YOUR HEAD AND BODY **PERFECTLY STILL** THROUGHOUT THE STROKE.

USUALLY, I CAN BEST ACHIEVE THAT ABSOLUTE PUTTING FUNDAMENTAL BY FEELING A PREDOMINANCE OF WEIGHT ON MY LEFT FOOT — AND PARTICULARLY ON THE **HEEL**.

EXPERIMENT TO DISCOVER THE SET-UP THAT GIVES YOU THE GREATEST **STABILITY** OVER THE BALL.

Look to Target from Behind Ball

I'LL VARY MY PUTTING STANCE A LITTLE FROM DAY TO DAY IN THE SEARCH FOR COMFORT. BUT BASICALLY I GET THE BEST RESULTS FROM REASONABLY SQUARE ALIGNMENT OF MY BODY TO THE TARGET LINE.

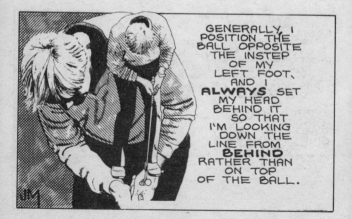

GENERALLY, I POSITION THE BALL OPPOSITE THE INSTEP OF MY LEFT FOOT, AND I **ALWAYS** SET MY HEAD BEHIND IT SO THAT I'M LOOKING DOWN THE LINE FROM **BEHIND** RATHER THAN ON TOP OF THE BALL.

Find Your Own Best Posture

HOW TALL OR CROUCHED YOU SET UP TO PUTT IS A MATTER OF PERSONAL PREFERENCE.

WATCH THE TOUR PROS AND YOU'LL SEE ALL SORTS OF STYLES, FROM VERY UPRIGHT TO ALMOST DOUBLED OVER.

I'M ESSENTIALLY A CROUCHER BECAUSE, BY GETTING WELL DOWN TO AND BEHIND THE BALL, I FEEL I CAN GET A BETTER SIGHTING OF THE LINE. WHICHEVER WAY YOU STAND, HOWEVER, BE SURE THAT YOUR EYES ARE **DEAD OVER** THE BALL AT ADDRESS, BECAUSE THAT'S FUNDAMENTAL TO ALMOST ALL FINE PUTTERS.

Check Your Right Elbow Position

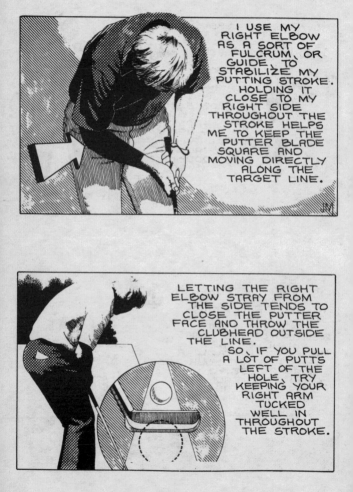

I USE MY RIGHT ELBOW AS A SORT OF FULCRUM, OR GUIDE, TO STABILIZE MY PUTTING STROKE. HOLDING IT CLOSE TO MY RIGHT SIDE THROUGHOUT THE STROKE HELPS ME TO KEEP THE PUTTER BLADE SQUARE AND MOVING DIRECTLY ALONG THE TARGET LINE.

LETTING THE RIGHT ELBOW STRAY FROM THE SIDE TENDS TO CLOSE THE PUTTER FACE AND THROW THE CLUBHEAD OUTSIDE THE LINE.

SO, IF YOU PULL A LOT OF PUTTS LEFT OF THE HOLE, TRY KEEPING YOUR RIGHT ARM TUCKED WELL IN THROUGHOUT THE STROKE.

IF YOU HAVE TROUBLE TAKING THE PUTTER AWAY SMOOTHLY, A FORWARD PRESS MIGHT HELP YOU DEVELOP A MORE FLUID START-BACK MOTION.

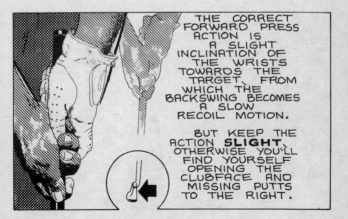

THE CORRECT FORWARD PRESS ACTION IS A SLIGHT INCLINATION OF THE WRISTS TOWARDS THE TARGET, FROM WHICH THE BACKSWING BECOMES A SLOW RECOIL MOTION.

BUT KEEP THE ACTION **SLIGHT**, OTHERWISE YOU'LL FIND YOURSELF OPENING THE CLUBFACE AND MISSING PUTTS TO THE RIGHT.

Swing Blade Low to Ground

TRUE END — OVER — END BALL ROLL IS THE FIRST GOAL IN PUTTING. THE **HEIGHT** OF YOUR STROKE HAS A BEARING ON THIS.

LIFTING THE CLUB ON THE BACKSWING CAUSES A CHOPPING — DOWN TYPE IMPACT THAT CREATES BACKSPIN (AND SOMETIMES ALSO SIDESPIN). LIFTING THE CLUB ON THE THROUGH — STROKE CREATES A SCOOPING TYPE ACTION THAT BREEDS "THIN" OR SEMI — TOPPED CONTACT. SO TRY TO KEEP THE BLADE AS LOW AS POSSIBLE BOTH SIDES OF THE BALL FOR A SQUARE, SOLID HIT.

Set-Up and Stroke to a Specific Plan

CONFIDENCE IS THE PRIMARY REQUIREMENT IN PUTTING.

IF YOU <u>THINK</u> YOU'LL MAKE A PUTT, YOU PROBABLY WILL.

IF YOU <u>DON'T</u> THINK YOU'LL MAKE IT, YOU ALMOST CERTAINLY WON'T.

PROPER PLANNING BREEDS CONFIDENCE.

STUDY LINE, BREAK AND SPEED, AND FORM A POSITIVE PICTURE IN YOUR MIND OF HOW THE BALL MUST BEHAVE TO DROP INTO THE HOLE.

THEN **STICK TO YOUR PLAN** AS YOU SET UP TO AND STROKE THE BALL.

6

Strategy and Tactics

Habitualize a "Reading" Routine

ALL GOOD GOLFERS DEVELOP A SET OF ROUTINES THAT BEST ENABLE THEM TO PREPARE PROPERLY FOR SHOTS. HERE'S MINE ON THE PUTTING GREEN.
FIRST, AS I WALK ONTO THE GREEN, I CHECK OVERALL SLOPE OF THE LAND, THE GRAIN DIRECTION, AND ANY WIND FACTOR.

NEXT, I ASSESS THE SPECIFIC ANGLES AND BREAKS BETWEEN BALL AND CUP, AT THE SAME TIME EXAMINING THE LENGTH AND TEXTURE OF THE GRASS TO DETERMINE THE PROPER SPEED OF THE PUTT.

FINALLY, I COMPUTE THESE FACTORS INTO A COMPLETE MENTAL PICTURE OF THE PUTT AS I STEP UP TO THE BALL.

"See" Ball Dropping as You Plan

I PUTT BEST WHEN I CAN ALMOST LITERALLY "SEE" THE BALL RUNNING TO AND DROPPING INTO THE CUP IN MY MIND'S EYE AS I PLAN THE SHOT.

CONFIDENCE IN ONE'S STROKE IS A PREREQUISITE TO PAINTING SUCH PRETTY PICTURES, BUT SO EQUALLY IS PROPER SURVEYING OF EACH AND EVERY PUTT. DON'T HOLD UP PLAY, BUT **DO** TAKE ENOUGH TIME TO PROPERLY IDENTIFY THE BALL'S LINE AND COMPUTE ITS SPEED. IDEALLY, DO THAT SURVEYING WHILE YOUR PLAYING PARTNERS ARE SUMMING UP THEIR PUTTS.

Make Your Own Decisions

FRIENDLY AND WELL-MEANING ADVICE IS USUALLY IN PLENTIFUL SUPPLY ON GOLF COURSES, ESPECIALLY ON THE GREENS FROM PLAYING PARTNERS AND CADDIES.

THIS, HOWEVER, IS A TIME TO "SHUT OUT THE WORLD" IN MY BOOK.

AS ALL PUTTS IN THE FINAL ANALYSIS ARE "SPEED" PUTTS, AND AS NO ONE ELSE KNOWS HOW HARD YOU ARE GOING TO HIT THE BALL, I DON'T SEE HOW THEY CAN EFFECTIVELY ADVISE ON BREAK OR ANY OTHER FACTORS.

SO BE A LONER ON THE GREENS — DO YOUR OWN READING, AS YOU MUST DO YOUR OWN STROKING.

JM

Squat for Best Angle on Slopes

STAND ERECT IN ASSESSING THE LINE OF THE PUTT AND THE MORE SUBTLE UNDULATIONS IN THE GREEN WILL TEND TO FLATTEN OUT.

LIE ON YOUR BELLY AND ALL YOU'LL SEE CLEARLY IS THE UPS AND DOWNS IN THE IMMEDIATE FOREGROUND.

THAT'S WHY I PREFER TO SQUAT OR BEND OVER FROM THE WAIST IN READING GREENS.

WITH MY HEAD AT ABOUT THREE FEET OFF THE GROUND, I SEEM TO GET THE BEST PERSPECTIVE ON BOTH SLOPE AND LINE, ESPECIALLY ON MIDDLE-DISTANCE PUTTS.

Focus Chiefly on Distance

WHAT'S MORE IMPORTANT IN PUTTING, **DIRECTION** OR **DISTANCE**? MOST PEOPLE CAN INTUITIVELY JUDGE THE LINE TO THE HOLE ON APPROACH PUTTS SUFFICIENTLY WELL TO STROKE THE BALL WITHIN REASONABLE PROXIMITY OF THE CUP. MANY, HOWEVER, SEEM TO HAVE MUCH GREATER PROBLEMS JUDGING DISTANCE.

IF YOU'RE ONE OF THOSE, AFTER HAVING DECIDED THE LINE, FIX YOUR MIND AS YOU PREPARE TO PUTT CHIEFLY ON **DISTANCE**, NOT DIRECTION. THINK LAST BEFORE YOU SWING ABOUT THE FORCE OR "WEIGHT" OF THE STROKE, TRYING TO SENSE IT IN YOUR HANDS AS YOU MAKE YOUR PRACTICE MOTIONS.

I THINK SO DOING WILL DEFINITELY CUT DOWN ON THOSE THREE-PUTT HORRORS.

Don't Be Over-Ambitious

SOME GREAT PUTTERS WILL TELL YOU THEY TRY TO HOLE EVERYTHING ON THE GREENS, BUT IT'S MY BELIEF THAT MOST TOUR PLAYERS, PUTTING FROM MORE THAN 30 OR SO FEET, ARE GENERALLY THINKING TWO PUTTS, NOT ONE.

TWO-FOOT RADIUS

DANGER IN BEING TOO AMBITIOUS IS OVER-HITTING THE PUTT AND THEN FACING A LONG ONE COMING BACK.

IT'S BETTER IN MY BOOK — UNLESS YOU ACTUALLY HAVE TO HOLE A "SNAKE" TO WIN — TO THINK OF GETTING THE BALL WITHIN A TWO-FOOT RADIUS OF THE CUP, RATHER THAN ACTUALLY IN THE HOLE.

AT LEAST, YOU'LL DEFINITELY THREE-PUTT LESS WITH SUCH AN APPROACH.

Never Overlook Grain Factors

ALMOST ALL TYPES OFF GRASS HAVE SOME DEGREE OF GRAIN, AND AN AWFUL LOT OF MAKEABLE PUTTS ARE MISSED BY GOLFERS WHO DON'T NOTICE IT OR KNOW HOW TO READ IT.

MOST GRASSES GROW EITHER TOWARD THE NEAREST WATER OR IN THE DIRECTION OF DRAINAGE. IN CERTAIN PARTS OF THE WORLD THEY GROW PREDOMINANTLY TOWARD THE SETTING SUN. ONE VISUAL TEST IS THE SHEEN OF THE GRASS. IF IT'S LIGHT AND SILVERY, THEN YOU'RE GENERALLY WITH THE GRAIN, AND IF IT'S DARK OR MATT-LOOKING THEN YOU'RE USUALLY AGAINST IT.

Know How Grain Influences Ball

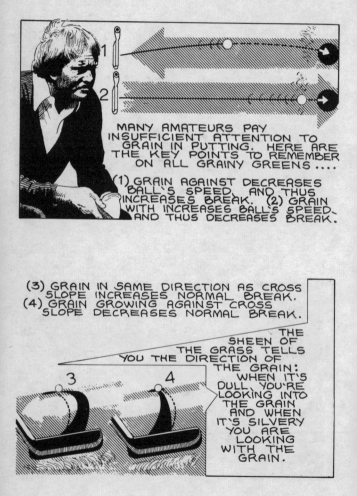

MANY AMATEURS PAY INSUFFICIENT ATTENTION TO GRAIN IN PUTTING. HERE ARE THE KEY POINTS TO REMEMBER ON ALL GRAINY GREENS....

(1) GRAIN AGAINST DECREASES BALL'S SPEED, AND THUS INCREASES BREAK. (2) GRAIN WITH INCREASES BALL'S SPEED, AND THUS DECREASES BREAK.

(3) GRAIN IN SAME DIRECTION AS CROSS SLOPE INCREASES NORMAL BREAK. (4) GRAIN GROWING AGAINST CROSS SLOPE DECREASES NORMAL BREAK.

THE SHEEN OF THE GRASS TELLS YOU THE DIRECTION OF THE GRAIN: WHEN IT'S DULL, YOU'RE LOOKING INTO THE GRAIN AND WHEN IT'S SILVERY YOU ARE LOOKING WITH THE GRAIN.

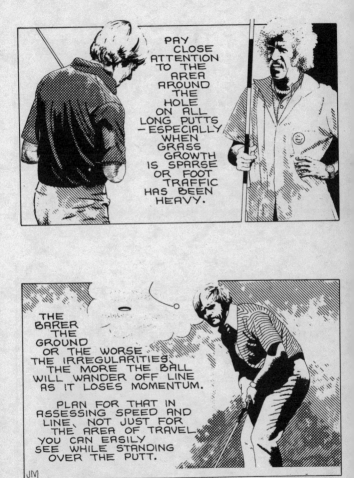

PAY CLOSE ATTENTION TO THE AREA AROUND THE HOLE ON ALL LONG PUTTS — ESPECIALLY WHEN GRASS GROWTH IS SPARSE OR FOOT TRAFFIC HAS BEEN HEAVY.

THE BARER THE GROUND OR THE WORSE THE IRREGULARITIES THE MORE THE BALL WILL WANDER OFF LINE AS IT LOSES MOMENTUM.

PLAN FOR THAT IN ASSESSING SPEED AND LINE, NOT JUST FOR THE AREA OF TRAVEL YOU CAN EASILY SEE WHILE STANDING OVER THE PUTT.

DOUBLE-BREAKING PUTTS NEED EXTRA CARE.

HERE'S A SYSTEM THAT MIGHT HELP YOU TAKE SOME OF THE COMPLEXITY OUT OF THEM.

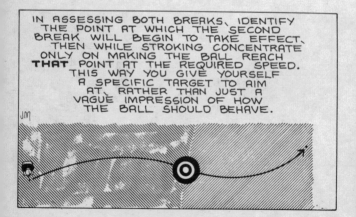

IN ASSESSING BOTH BREAKS, IDENTIFY THE POINT AT WHICH THE SECOND BREAK WILL BEGIN TO TAKE EFFECT. THEN WHILE STROKING CONCENTRATE ONLY ON MAKING THE BALL REACH **THAT** POINT AT THE REQUIRED SPEED. THIS WAY YOU GIVE YOURSELF A SPECIFIC TARGET TO AIM AT, RATHER THAN JUST A VAGUE IMPRESSION OF HOW THE BALL SHOULD BEHAVE.

OCCASIONALLY YOU WILL ENCOUNTER A PUTT WHERE THE BREAK APPEARS TO DIFFER GREATLY WHEN VIEWED FROM OPPOSITE SIDES OF THE HOLE.

THE BEST ANSWER TO THIS CONFUSING SITUATION LIES IN THE SURROUNDING TERRAIN.
GENERALLY, YOU'LL FIND THE BALL MORE LIKELY TO TURN **WITH** THE GENERAL SLOPE THAN AGAINST IT.
SO LOOK AROUND AT THE OVERALL LIE OF THE LAND BEFORE YOU MAKE A DECISION.

Take Relief from Standing Water

DEMANDING AS THEY MAY SOMETIMES SEEM TO BE, ONE THING THE **R**ULES OF **G**OLF DON'T REQUIRE YOU TO DO IS PLAY FROM OR THROUGH STANDING WATER — UNLESS YOU'VE LANDED IN AN ACTUAL WATER HAZARD, THAT IS.

BE AWARE OF THIS ON THE GREENS AS WELL AS 'THROUGH THE GREEN.'

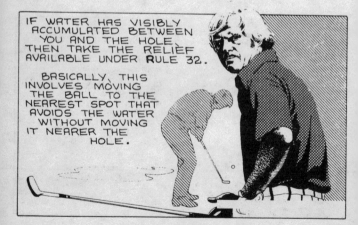

IF WATER HAS VISIBLY ACCUMULATED BETWEEN YOU AND THE HOLE, THEN TAKE THE RELIEF AVAILABLE UNDER **R**ULE 32.

BASICALLY, THIS INVOLVES MOVING THE BALL TO THE NEAREST SPOT THAT AVOIDS THE WATER WITHOUT MOVING IT NEARER THE HOLE.

Don't Let Moisture Fool You

DON'T LET MOISTURE FOOL YOU ON THE GREENS. THERE ARE TWO TYPES — RECOGNIZE THE DIFFERENCE.

WHEN THE GROUND ITSELF IS THOROUGHLY SOAKED, THE BALL WILL NEITHER ROLL NOR BREAK AS MUCH AS NORMAL, THUS REQUIRING A **FIRMER** STROKE.

WHEN THE GROUND IS BASICALLY FIRM, BUT THE SURFACE HAS BEEN DAMPENED BY DEW OR A SHOWER, THE BALL GENERALLY WILL BOTH ROLL AND BREAK ALMOST AS MUCH AS IN DRY CONDITIONS.

SO HIT PRETTY MUCH WHAT YOU SEE IN TERMS OF BREAK, AND GO EASY ON THE POWER.

Play to Putt Out Uphill on Fast Greens

HERE'S A TIP THAT WILL HELP YOU ANY TIME YOU PUTT VERY FAST GREENS.

IN THINKING DISTANCE, PLAN TO LEAVE YOURSELF AN **UPHILL** PUTT SHOULD YOU MISS THE HOLE ON THE PRESENT ATTEMPT.

ON VERY SLICK GREENS I'D RATHER HAVE EVEN A SIDEHILL PUTT THAN ONE GOING STRAIGHT DOWN A PRONOUNCED SLOPE, BECAUSE THOSE "SLIDERS" ARE THE TRICKIEST TO JUDGE AND STROKE IN THE GAME.

SO PLAN CAREFULLY SLOPE-WISE, ESPECIALLY ON LONG APPROACH PUTTS — AND ON CHIP SHOTS, TOO.

Try This Tactic on Short Downhillers

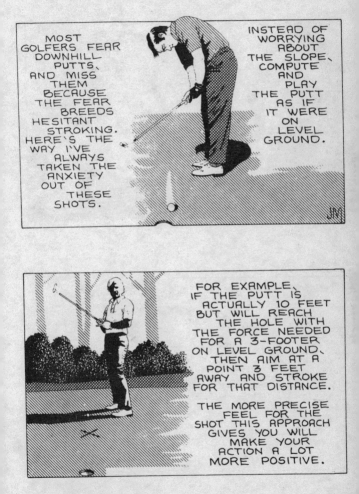

MOST GOLFERS FEAR DOWNHILL PUTTS, AND MISS THEM BECAUSE THE FEAR BREEDS HESITANT STROKING. HERE'S THE WAY I'VE ALWAYS TAKEN THE ANXIETY OUT OF THESE SHOTS.

INSTEAD OF WORRYING ABOUT THE SLOPE, COMPUTE AND PLAY THE PUTT AS IF IT WERE ON LEVEL GROUND.

FOR EXAMPLE, IF THE PUTT IS ACTUALLY 10 FEET BUT WILL REACH THE HOLE WITH THE FORCE NEEDED FOR A 3-FOOTER ON LEVEL GROUND, THEN AIM AT A POINT 3 FEET AWAY AND STROKE FOR THAT DISTANCE.

THE MORE PRECISE FEEL FOR THE SHOT THIS APPROACH GIVES YOU WILL MAKE YOUR ACTION A LOT MORE POSITIVE.

Be Firm on Short Uphillers

GOLF IS A GAME OF PERCENTAGES. BEING **FIRM** ON SHORT UP-HILLERS PUTS THEM IN YOUR FAVOR, BOTH BECAUSE THERE IS LITTLE DANGER OF RUNNING A LONG WAY PAST, AND BECAUSE THE HIGHER REAR EDGE OF THE HOLE MAKES FOR A BETTER BACKSTOP.

REMEMBER THAT THE FASTER IT TRAVELS, THE LESS THE BALL WILL BREAK.

SO ALLOW FOR A LITTLE LESS CURVE THAN YOU WOULD IF YOU WERE 'DIEING' THE BALL INTO THE HOLE.

FIRM

DIEING

JM

Make Hole Look Like a Bucket

IF YOU'RE SUFFERING FROM PUTTING BLUES, TRY PRACTICING TO A **TEE** STUCK IN THE GROUND INSTEAD OF TO A HOLE.

BY MAKING YOU LESS "CUP CONSCIOUS," THIS WILL HELP YOU CONCENTRATE BETTER ON STROKE MECHANICS AND TEMPO. ALSO, ONCE YOU GET BACK ON THE COURSE, THE HOLE WILL LOOK LIKE A BUCKET!

SMOOTHNESS..

Practice the Putts You Plan to Hole

WATCHING AMATEURS PRACTICE BEFORE PRO-AMS, I OFTEN SEE THEM PUTTING CONTINUOUSLY FROM 40 FEET OR MORE.

I SOMETIMES WONDER HOW MANY SUCH MONSTERS THEY ACTUALLY EXPECT TO HOLE.

JM

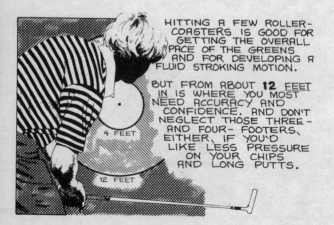

HITTING A FEW ROLLER-COASTERS IS GOOD FOR GETTING THE OVERALL PACE OF THE GREENS AND FOR DEVELOPING A FLUID STROKING MOTION.

BUT FROM ABOUT **12 FEET IN** IS WHERE YOU MOST NEED ACCURACY AND CONFIDENCE. AND DON'T NEGLECT THOSE THREE- AND FOUR-FOOTERS, EITHER, IF YOU'D LIKE LESS PRESSURE ON YOUR CHIPS AND LONG PUTTS.

4 FEET

12 FEET

N MATCH-PLAY, DON'T TRY TO BE A HERO ON THE GREENS WHEN THERE IS NO NEED FOR HEROICS.

IF YOUR OPPONENT IS 20 FEET AWAY AND YOU ARE 40 FEET, WORK AT LAGGING YOUR PUTT "DEAD" RATHER THAN RISKING THREE-PUTTING BY TRYING TO HOLE IT.

JUST GET IT CLOSE!

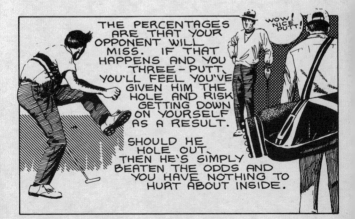

THE PERCENTAGES ARE THAT YOUR OPPONENT WILL MISS. IF THAT HAPPENS AND YOU THREE-PUTT, YOU'LL FEEL YOU'VE GIVEN HIM THE HOLE AND RISK GETTING DOWN ON YOURSELF AS A RESULT.

SHOULD HE HOLE OUT, THEN HE'S SIMPLY BEATEN THE ODDS AND YOU HAVE NOTHING TO HURT ABOUT INSIDE.

WOW! NICE PUTT!

7

Faults and
Cures

Accelerate *the Putterhead*

KNOW WHY YOU'RE MISSING ALL THOSE MAKABLE PUTTS? YOU'RE TAKING TOO LONG A BACKSWING, WHICH CAUSES YOU TO <u>DECELERATE</u> ON THE THROUGH-SWING.

PRACTICING WITH AN OBJECT ABOUT THREE INCHES BEHIND THE PUTTERHEAD WILL FORCE YOU TO SHORTEN YOUR BACKSWING.

THEN, EXAGGERATING YOUR FOLLOW-THROUGH WILL HELP YOU ACCELERATE THE PUTTERHEAD <u>THROUGH</u>, NOT JUST <u>TO</u>, THE BALL.

Change Grip to Stop Pulling

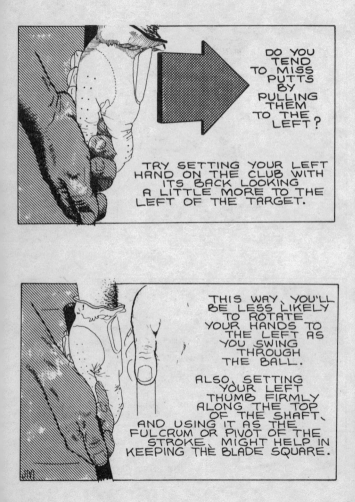

DO YOU TEND TO MISS PUTTS BY PULLING THEM TO THE LEFT?

TRY SETTING YOUR LEFT HAND ON THE CLUB WITH ITS BACK LOOKING A LITTLE MORE TO THE LEFT OF THE TARGET.

THIS WAY, YOU'LL BE LESS LIKELY TO ROTATE YOUR HANDS TO THE LEFT AS YOU SWING THROUGH THE BALL.

ALSO, SETTING YOUR LEFT THUMB FIRMLY ALONG THE TOP OF THE SHAFT, AND USING IT AS THE FULCRUM OR PIVOT OF THE STROKE, MIGHT HELP IN KEEPING THE BLADE SQUARE.

Watch Blade to Correct Mishits

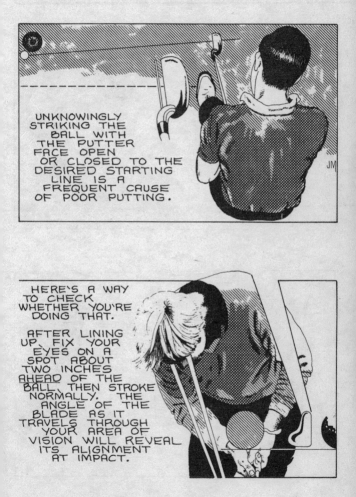

UNKNOWINGLY STRIKING THE BALL WITH THE PUTTER FACE OPEN OR CLOSED TO THE DESIRED STARTING LINE IS A FREQUENT CAUSE OF POOR PUTTING.

HERE'S A WAY TO CHECK WHETHER YOU'RE DOING THAT.

AFTER LINING UP, FIX YOUR EYES ON A SPOT ABOUT TWO INCHES AHEAD OF THE BALL, THEN STROKE NORMALLY. THE ANGLE OF THE BLADE AS IT TRAVELS THROUGH YOUR AREA OF VISION WILL REVEAL ITS ALIGNMENT AT IMPACT.

Try More Backswing, Not More Force

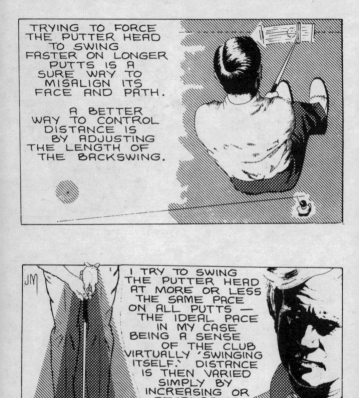

TRYING TO FORCE THE PUTTER HEAD TO SWING FASTER ON LONGER PUTTS IS A SURE WAY TO MISALIGN ITS FACE AND PATH.

A BETTER WAY TO CONTROL DISTANCE IS BY ADJUSTING THE LENGTH OF THE BACKSWING.

I TRY TO SWING THE PUTTER HEAD AT MORE OR LESS THE SAME PACE ON ALL PUTTS — THE IDEAL PACE IN MY CASE BEING A SENSE OF THE CLUB VIRTUALLY 'SWINGING ITSELF.' DISTANCE IS THEN VARIED SIMPLY BY INCREASING OR DECREASING THE LENGTH OF THE BACKSWING.

IF YOU'RE LEAVING LONG PUTTS SHORT OR JERKING SHORT ONES OFF LINE, CHECK YOUR FOLLOW-THROUGH. IT'S JUST AS ESSENTIAL IN PUTTING AS ON WOOD AND IRON SHOTS.

DRAW AN IMAGINERY LINE ALONG THE STARTING PATH OF THE PUTT AND TRY TO CARRY THE PUTTER BLADE STRAIGHT ALONG IT AFTER IMPACT FOR AT LEAST FIVE OR SIX INCHES. YOU'LL STRIKE THE BALL MORE FIRMLY AND SQUARELY BY **ACCELERATING** THROUGH IT BETTER.

Let Putterhead Do the Work

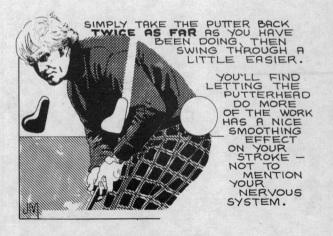

Stay on Path to Drop Those Shorties

IF YOU'RE MISSING A LOT OF SHORT PUTTS, TRY MAKING A CONSCIOUS — EVEN EXAGGERATED — FOLLOW-THROUGH ALONG THE PATH YOU WANT THE BALL TO TAKE.

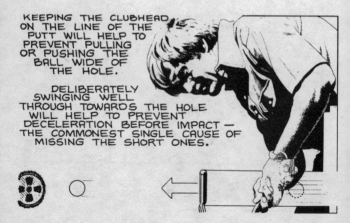

KEEPING THE CLUBHEAD ON THE LINE OF THE PUTT WILL HELP TO PREVENT PULLING OR PUSHING THE BALL WIDE OF THE HOLE.

DELIBERATELY SWINGING WELL THROUGH TOWARDS THE HOLE WILL HELP TO PREVENT DECELERATION BEFORE IMPACT — THE COMMONEST SINGLE CAUSE OF MISSING THE SHORT ONES.

Part THREE

Managing Your Game from Tee to Green

8

Fundamentals of
Good Strategy

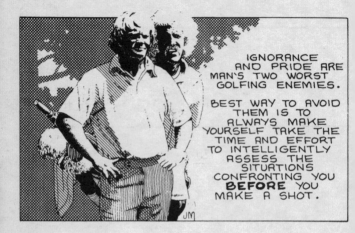

IGNORANCE AND PRIDE ARE MAN'S TWO WORST GOLFING ENEMIES.

BEST WAY TO AVOID THEM IS TO ALWAYS MAKE YOURSELF TAKE THE TIME AND EFFORT TO INTELLIGENTLY ASSESS THE SITUATIONS CONFRONTING YOU **BEFORE** YOU MAKE A SHOT.

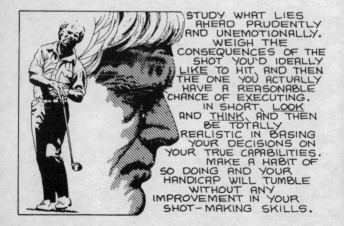

STUDY WHAT LIES AHEAD PRUDENTLY AND UNEMOTIONALLY. WEIGH THE CONSEQUENCES OF THE SHOT YOU'D IDEALLY LIKE TO HIT, AND THEN THE ONE YOU ACTUALLY HAVE A REASONABLE CHANCE OF EXECUTING. IN SHORT, LOOK AND THINK, AND THEN BE TOTALLY REALISTIC IN BASING YOUR DECISIONS ON YOUR TRUE CAPABILITIES. MAKE A HABIT OF SO DOING AND YOUR HANDICAP WILL TUMBLE WITHOUT ANY IMPROVEMENT IN YOUR SHOT-MAKING SKILLS.

"Blank Out" the Bad Shots

TOO OFTEN ONE BAD GOLF SHOT IMMEDIATELY LEADS TO ANOTHER AT LEAST AS BAD OR EVEN WORSE. THE REASON IS ALMOST ALWAYS ANGER AND FRUSTRATION, NOT SUDDEN LOSS OF SWING SKILLS.

I'VE GENERALLY MANAGED TO AVOID THIS TRAP BY "BLANKING OUT" THE BAD SHOT BY CONSCIOUSLY FORCING MY MIND TO FOCUS IMMEDIATELY ON THE RECOVERY I NOW HAVE TO PLAY. IN OTHER WORDS, I SWITCH OFF THE FAULT AND SWITCH ON TO THE REMEDY AS FAST AS I POSSIBLY CAN. IT TAKES DISCIPLINE, BUT IT ALSO PAYS BIG DIVIDENDS.

A COUPLE OF FRIENDS MENTIONED RECENTLY THAT THEY PLAYED MUCH BETTER UPON FIRST COMING BACK FROM A LAY-OFF THAN WHEN THEY WERE TEEING IT UP REGULARLY. I DON'T THINK THE REASON IS HARD TO GUESS.

JM

PLAYING FREQUENTLY, YOU PUT YOURSELF UNDER PRESSURE TO PLAY WELL, WHICH BREEDS BOTH MENTAL AND PHYSICAL TENSION.

NOT EXPECTING TO DO MUCH AFTER A LAY-OFF, YOU'RE **RELAXED** — AND YOU PLAY WELL AS A RESULT.

IF THAT'S AS TRUE AS I THINK IT IS, THEN OBVIOUSLY ANYTHING YOU CAN DO TO **STAY** RELAXED ONCE YOU'RE BACK IS GOING TO MAKE YOU A BETTER PLAYER.

Work on Your "Vizualization"

IF YOU GENERALLY STRIKE THE BALL PRETTY WELL BUT FALL SHORT, LONG OR WIDE OF A LOT OF TARGETS, DO SOME WORK ON YOUR VISUALIZATION PROCESSES <u>BEFORE</u> YOU HIT — AND, PREFERABLY, EVEN BEFORE YOU SELECT A CLUB.

START BY FULLY ANALYZING ALL THE FACTORS THAT WILL DECIDE THE TYPE OF SHOT YOU'LL PLAY. NEXT, VISUALIZE THAT SPECIFIC SHOT FLYING TO YOUR TARGET — ACTUALLY "SEE" IT IN YOUR MIND'S EYE. FINALLY, IMAGINE AND MENTALLY "FEEL" THE SWING YOU NEED TO MAKE THE SHOT. ONLY THEN DRAW OUT A CLUB AND GO INTO ACTION.

Think "Target," Not "Trouble"

THINK **TARGET**, NOT "TROUBLE," IN SETTING UP TO EVERY SHOT.

BLOT OUT THE POTENTIAL HAZARDS BY CONCENTRATING HARD ON THE AREA YOU WANT TO HIT, NOT THOSE YOU WANT TO MISS.

OVER-CONSCIOUSNESS OF HAZARDS IS A PRIME CAUSE OF BOTH MUSCULAR TENSION AND TRYING TO "GUIDE" THE BALL AMONG WEEKEND GOLFERS. THINK ONLY OF THE RESULTS YOU SEEK AND YOU WILL BOTH AIM AND ALIGN MORE ACCURATELY AND SWING MORE FREELY.

Go with Your Natural "Shape"

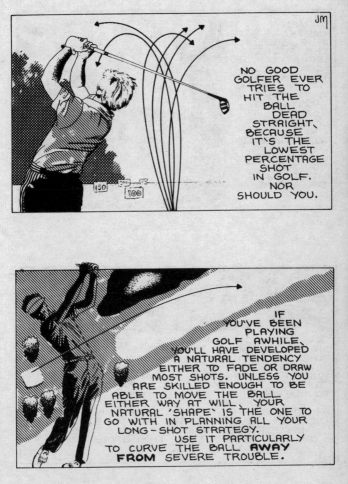

NO GOOD GOLFER EVER TRIES TO HIT THE BALL DEAD STRAIGHT, BECAUSE IT'S THE LOWEST PERCENTAGE SHOT IN GOLF. NOR SHOULD YOU.

IF YOU'VE BEEN PLAYING GOLF AWHILE, YOU'LL HAVE DEVELOPED A NATURAL TENDENCY EITHER TO FADE OR DRAW MOST SHOTS. UNLESS YOU ARE SKILLED ENOUGH TO BE ABLE TO MOVE THE BALL EITHER WAY AT WILL, YOUR NATURAL 'SHAPE' IS THE ONE TO GO WITH IN PLANNING ALL YOUR LONG-SHOT STRATEGY.

USE IT PARTICULARLY TO CURVE THE BALL **AWAY FROM** SEVERE TROUBLE.

MANY AMATEURS SLICE THE BALL TO THE RIGHT REPEATEDLY, BUT CONTINUALLY AIM STRAIGHT IN THE HOPE THAT **THIS TIME** IT WILL FLY STRAIGHT.

UNFORTUNATELY, THEIR OPTIMISM FAR EXCEEDS THE LAWS OF CHANCE.

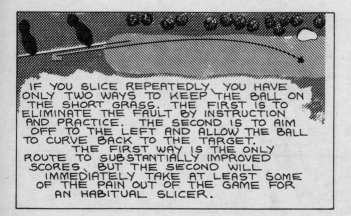

IF YOU SLICE REPEATEDLY, YOU HAVE ONLY TWO WAYS TO KEEP THE BALL ON THE SHORT GRASS. THE FIRST IS TO ELIMINATE THE FAULT BY INSTRUCTION AND PRACTICE. THE SECOND IS TO AIM OFF TO THE LEFT AND ALLOW THE BALL TO CURVE BACK TO THE TARGET.

THE FIRST WAY IS THE ONLY ROUTE TO SUBSTANTIALLY IMPROVED SCORES, BUT THE SECOND WILL IMMEDIATELY TAKE AT LEAST SOME OF THE PAIN OUT OF THE GAME FOR AN HABITUAL SLICER.

Play the Percentages

MY APPROACH TO TROUBLE IS TO GAMBLE AS MUCH AS POSSIBLE WITHOUT BEING FLAT-OUT FOOLISH. FOR EXAMPLE, IF I'M IN A DENSE FOREST AND THERE IS OUT-OF-BOUNDS OR WATER CLOSE BY, I'LL PLAY THE SAFEST POSSIBLE "GET OUT" SHOT.

HOWEVER, IF I'M BEHIND JUST A FEW TREES WITH NOT MUCH OTHER TROUBLE AROUND, I'LL USUALLY TRY TO WORK THE BALL THROUGH AN OPENING, THE PERCENTAGES BEING THAT I'LL HAVE AS GOOD A NEXT SHOT AS I'D HAVE HAD BY CHIPPING OUT, EVEN IF I DO CATCH SOME PART OF THE WOODWORK.

Beware Those Easy-Looking Holes

DON'T LET THE FACT THAT A HOLE IS COMPARATIVELY SHORT OR SIMPLE-LOOKING LET YOU TAKE IT FOR GRANTED.

FOR EXAMPLE, NO. 7 AT AUGUSTA NATIONAL IS ONLY 365 YARDS LONG AND STRAIGHT-AWAY FROM TEE TO GREEN, BUT IT'S ACTUALLY ONE OF THE TOUGHEST PAR-FOURS IN CHAMPIONSHIP GOLF.

THE NARROW, TREE-LINED FAIRWAY DEMANDS GREAT ACCURACY FROM THE TEE, BUT YOU ALSO NEED GOOD DISTANCE SO AS TO BE ABLE TO THROW A HIGH, SOFT SHOT INTO THE VERY SHALLOW, SAND-SURROUNDED, STEEPLY-ANGLED GREEN.

IN OTHER WORDS, LIKE A LOT OF SHORT PAR FOURS, THIS EASY-LOOKING HOLE ACTUALLY DEMANDS MAXIMUM THINKING AND STRIKING EFFORT ON EVERY SHOT.

JM

Take It Easy After a Lay-Off

STARTING GOLF AGAIN AFTER A LONG LAYOFF?

DON'T GO OUT THE FIRST TIME AND BEAT A THOUSAND RANGE BALLS: YOUR MUSCLES AREN'T READY FOR IT AND THEY WILL DEFINITELY PUNISH YOU!

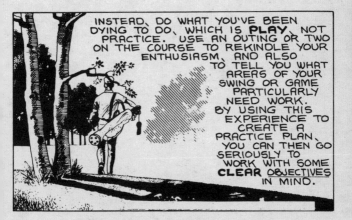

INSTEAD, DO WHAT YOU'VE BEEN DYING TO DO, WHICH IS **PLAY**, NOT PRACTICE. USE AN OUTING OR TWO ON THE COURSE TO REKINDLE YOUR ENTHUSIASM, AND ALSO TO TELL YOU WHAT AREAS OF YOUR SWING OR GAME PARTICULARLY NEED WORK. BY USING THIS EXPERIENCE TO CREATE A PRACTICE PLAN, YOU CAN THEN GO SERIOUSLY TO WORK WITH SOME **CLEAR** OBJECTIVES IN MIND.

9

From
the Tee

Never Rush the Opening Drive

ONE OF GOLF'S MOST IMPORTANT SHOTS IS THE OPENING DRIVE.

HIT IT WELL AND ALL SEEMS RIGHT WITH THE WORLD. HIT IT POORLY AND, AS LIKE AS NOT, YOU'VE SET THE TONE FOR A FRUSTRATING DAY.

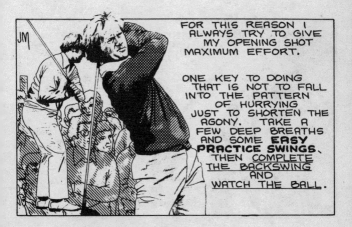

FOR THIS REASON I ALWAYS TRY TO GIVE MY OPENING SHOT MAXIMUM EFFORT.

ONE KEY TO DOING THAT IS NOT TO FALL INTO THE PATTERN OF HURRYING JUST TO SHORTEN THE AGONY. TAKE A FEW DEEP BREATHS AND SOME **EASY PRACTICE SWINGS**, THEN <u>COMPLETE THE BACKSWING</u> AND <u>WATCH THE BALL</u>.

IN PLANNING TEE SHOTS, DON'T THINK OF THINGS TO AVOID LIKE WOODS OR BUNKERS. INSTEAD, IDENTIFY AND THEN MENTALLY FOCUS ON THE AREA OF THE FAIRWAY **YOU WANT TO HIT.**

HAVING DONE THAT, PICTURE THE SHOT THAT WILL GET YOU THERE IN YOUR MIND'S EYE, THEN MENTALLY REHEARSE THE SWING THAT WILL EXECUTE THE IMAGINED SHOT.

IN OTHER WORDS THINK **POSITIVELY,** NEVER NEGATIVELY, IN YOUR SHOT-PLANNING.

Be Observant

IT'S IMPOSSIBLE TO PLAY FOR POSITION FROM THE TEE IF YOU DON'T KNOW WHERE THE PIN IS LOCATED ON THE GREEN.

CADDIES SUPPLY THIS INFORMATION TO TOUR PLAYERS. IF THAT'S BEYOND YOUR RESOURCES, THEN AT LEAST BE SURE TO CHECK PIN LOCATIONS ON UPCOMING HOLES AS YOU PASS ADJACENT TO THEM OR WHENEVER THEY BECOME VISIBLE.

IN OTHER WORDS, BE OBSERVANT.

NO. 3
375 YDS.
PAR 4

Don't Fret About Being Out-Hit

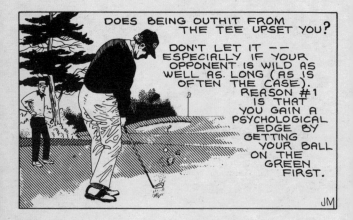

DOES BEING OUTHIT FROM THE TEE UPSET YOU?

DON'T LET IT -- ESPECIALLY IF YOUR OPPONENT IS WILD AS WELL AS. LONG (AS IS OFTEN THE CASE). REASON #1 IS THAT YOU GAIN A PSYCHOLOGICAL EDGE BY GETTING YOUR BALL ON THE GREEN FIRST.

JM

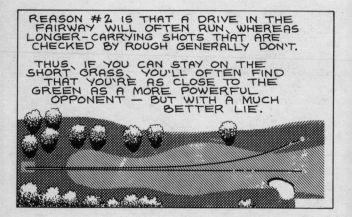

REASON #2 IS THAT A DRIVE IN THE FAIRWAY WILL OFTEN RUN, WHEREAS LONGER-CARRYING SHOTS THAT ARE CHECKED BY ROUGH GENERALLY DON'T.

THUS, IF YOU CAN STAY ON THE SHORT GRASS, YOU'LL OFTEN FIND THAT YOU'RE AS CLOSE TO THE GREEN AS A MORE POWERFUL OPPONENT — BUT WITH A MUCH BETTER LIE.

Put Position Ahead of Distance

DISTANCE IS VALUABLE IN GOLF, BUT ONLY IN TERMS OF MAKING THE NEXT SHOT EASIER — NEVER FOR ITS OWN SAKE.

EVEN MORE IMPORTANT IS POSITION — FOR EXAMPLE, A 7-IRON FROM A DOWNHILL/SIDEHILL LIE IS A TOUGHER SHOT THAN A 5-IRON FROM A LEVEL LIE.

SO DON'T JUST WHACK AWAY FROM THE TEE — REMEMBER THAT NEARNESS TO THE HOLE DOESN'T ALWAYS SET UP THE BEST APPROACH SITUATION.

EVEN IF YOU'RE NOT A GOOD ENOUGH STRIKER TO FREQUENTLY HIT A SPECIFIC AREA OF THE FAIRWAY, I STILL THINK YOU SHOULD **TRY** TO DO SO ON EVERY TEE SHOT.

WHY? BECAUSE THE MORE SPECIFICALLY YOU "TARGET" MENTALLY, THE MORE ACCURATELY YOU WILL PHYSICALLY AIM THE CLUBFACE AND ALIGN YOURSELF AT ADDRESS. AND THE MORE PRECISELY YOU DO BOTH THOSE THINGS, THE BETTER YOUR CHANCES OF HITTING THE BALL WHERE YOU'D LIKE IT TO GO.

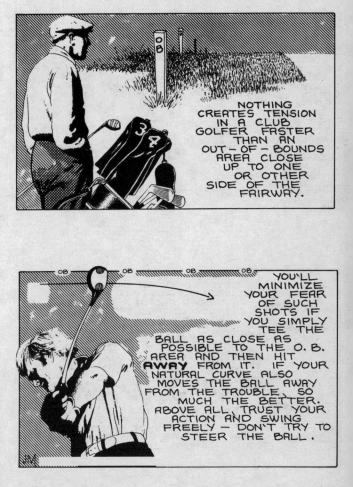

NOTHING CREATES TENSION IN A CLUB GOLFER FASTER THAN AN OUT-OF-BOUNDS AREA CLOSE UP TO ONE OR OTHER SIDE OF THE FAIRWAY.

YOU'LL MINIMIZE YOUR FEAR OF SUCH SHOTS IF YOU SIMPLY TEE THE BALL AS CLOSE AS POSSIBLE TO THE O.B. AREA AND THEN HIT **AWAY** FROM IT. IF YOUR NATURAL CURVE ALSO MOVES THE BALL AWAY FROM THE TROUBLE, SO MUCH THE BETTER. ABOVE ALL, TRUST YOUR ACTION AND SWING FREELY — DON'T TRY TO STEER THE BALL.

Beware the "Driver Syndrome"

COULD YOU GET MY DRIVER, PLEASE..

BEWARE THE SYNDROME OF **ALWAYS** HITTING A DRIVER SIMPLY BECAUSE A HOLE IS A PAR-4 OR A PAR-5. GET INTO THE HABIT OF LOOKING AT AND THINKING ABOUT WHAT LIES IMMEDIATELY AHEAD BEFORE SELECTING A TEE-SHOT CLUB.

NO. 7
355 YDS
PAR 4

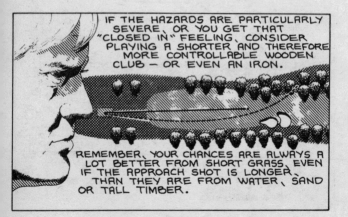

IF THE HAZARDS ARE PARTICULARLY SEVERE, OR YOU GET THAT "CLOSED IN" FEELING, CONSIDER PLAYING A SHORTER AND THEREFORE MORE CONTROLLABLE WOODEN CLUB — OR EVEN AN IRON.

REMEMBER, YOUR CHANCES ARE ALWAYS A LOT BETTER FROM SHORT GRASS, EVEN IF THE APPROACH SHOT IS LONGER, THAN THEY ARE FROM WATER, SAND OR TALL TIMBER.

Play Short of Severe Hazards

CONSIDER GOING WITH LESS THAN YOUR MAXIMUM-DISTANCE TEE-SHOT WHENEVER THERE IS POTENTIAL TREE TROUBLE UP AHEAD.

FOR EXAMPLE, IF THERE ARE A COUPLE OF TREES TO ONE SIDE OF THE FAIRWAY, A WELL-HIT BUT SLIGHTLY OFF-LINE DRIVE MIGHT PUT YOU SO CLOSE THAT YOU CAN NEITHER GO OVER OR AROUND THEM. A THREE- OR FOUR-WOOD FROM THE TEE, ON THE OTHER HAND, COULD LEAVE YOU FAR ENOUGH BACK TO TAKE ONE OF THOSE OPTIONS AND STILL GET HOME.

3-WOOD

DRIVER

Make Fairway Slopes Work for You

DON'T HAUL OFF AND FIRE CASUALLY TO A SLOPING FAIRWAY, ESPECIALLY IN DRY OR RUNNING GROUND CONDITIONS. MAKE THE SLOPE WORK **FOR**, NOT AGAINST YOU.

FOR EXAMPLE, IF THE LANDING AREA SLOPES UP FROM RIGHT TO LEFT, TRY EITHER TO DRAW THE BALL INTO IT OR AIM TO THE LEFT SIDE. CONVERSELY, PLAY A FADE OR AIM TO THE RIGHT SIDE OF THE FAIRWAY IN A LEFT-TO-RIGHT UP-SLOPING SITUATION. IN OTHER WORDS, BE OBSERVANT AND PLAN THE BEST PERCENTAGE SHOT <u>BEFORE</u> YOU SWING.

Tackle Dog-Legs This Way

A BASIC RULE OF DOG-LEG STRATEGY IS TO TRY TO "BEND" THE TEE-SHOT **WITH** RATHER THAN AGAINST THE FAIRWAY ANGLE: IN OTHER WORDS, FADE AROUND A LEFT-TO-RIGHT DOG-LEG, AND DRAW ON A RIGHT-TO-LEFT CURVE.

HOWEVER, IF YOU'RE TRYING TO CUT THE CORNER BY PLAYING <u>OVER</u> TREES OR OTHER "ELBOW" TROUBLE, THEN **REVERSING** THIS STRATEGY CAN GIVE YOU A LITTLE INSURANCE BY MOVING THE BALL AWAY FROM THE TROUBLE.

Position Ball for Solid Strike

HOW HIGH SHOULD YOU TEE THE BALL INTO A HEADWIND?

MY ADVICE IS HIGH ENOUGH TO BE SURE OF GETTING ALL OF THE **CLUBFACE** ON IT.

REMEMBER, THE PRIME REQUIREMENT HERE IS A TRULY **SOLID** HIT, MUCH MORE THAN A LOW FLIGHT.

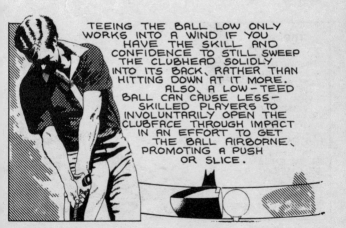

TEEING THE BALL LOW ONLY WORKS INTO A WIND IF YOU HAVE THE SKILL AND CONFIDENCE TO STILL SWEEP THE CLUBHEAD SOLIDLY INTO ITS BACK, RATHER THAN HITTING DOWN AT IT MORE. ALSO, A LOW-TEED BALL CAN CAUSE LESS-SKILLED PLAYERS TO INVOLUNTARILY OPEN THE CLUBFACE THROUGH IMPACT IN AN EFFORT TO GET THE BALL AIRBORNE, PROMOTING A PUSH OR SLICE.

Peg Ball on All Tee Shots

TEE THE BALL ON A PEG EVEN WHEN YOU'RE PLAYING IRON SHOTS TO PAR-THREE HOLES.

I USUALLY SET THE BALL ABOUT ¼ INCH ABOVE THE GROUND FOR A SHORT IRON SHOT, AND ABOUT ½ INCH UP FOR A LONG IRON.

NO. 4
156 YDS.
PAR 3

TEEING THE BALL NOT ONLY INCREASES YOUR CHANCE OF STRIKING IT SOLIDLY, BUT ALSO MINIMIZES THE RISK OF HITTING A "FLIER" AS THE RESULT OF GRASS INTERVENING BETWEEN THE BALL AND CLUB-FACE. ALWAYS TAKE ADVANTAGE OF SUCH "PERCENTAGES."

Don't "Reload" Too Hastily

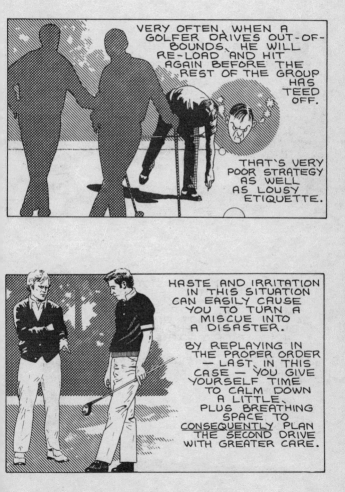

VERY OFTEN, WHEN A GOLFER DRIVES OUT-OF-BOUNDS, HE WILL RE-LOAD AND HIT AGAIN BEFORE THE REST OF THE GROUP HAS TEED OFF.

THAT'S VERY POOR STRATEGY AS WELL AS LOUSY ETIQUETTE.

HASTE AND IRRITATION IN THIS SITUATION CAN EASILY CAUSE YOU TO TURN A MISCUE INTO A DISASTER.

BY REPLAYING IN THE PROPER ORDER — LAST, IN THIS CASE — YOU GIVE YOURSELF TIME TO CALM DOWN A LITTLE, PLUS BREATHING SPACE TO <u>CONSEQUENTLY</u> PLAN THE SECOND DRIVE WITH GREATER CARE.

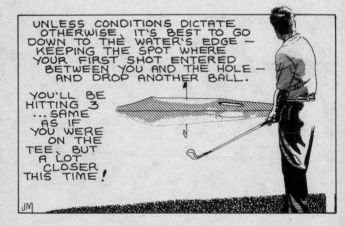

Never Drive without a Plan

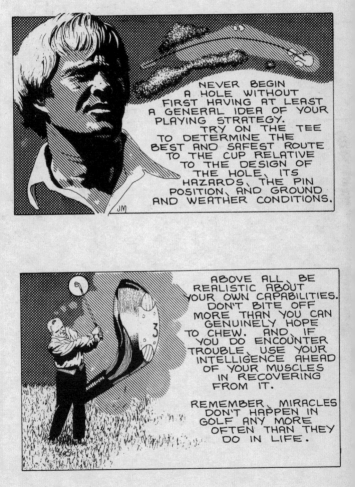

NEVER BEGIN A HOLE WITHOUT FIRST HAVING AT LEAST A GENERAL IDEA OF YOUR PLAYING STRATEGY. TRY ON THE TEE TO DETERMINE THE BEST AND SAFEST ROUTE TO THE CUP RELATIVE TO THE DESIGN OF THE HOLE, ITS HAZARDS, THE PIN POSITION, AND GROUND AND WEATHER CONDITIONS.

ABOVE ALL, BE REALISTIC ABOUT YOUR OWN CAPABILITIES. DON'T BITE OFF MORE THAN YOU CAN GENUINELY HOPE TO CHEW. AND IF YOU DO ENCOUNTER TROUBLE, USE YOUR INTELLIGENCE AHEAD OF YOUR MUSCLES IN RECOVERING FROM IT.

REMEMBER, MIRACLES DON'T HAPPEN IN GOLF ANY MORE OFTEN THAN THEY DO IN LIFE.

10

Into the
Green

Know How Far You Hit Each Club

HERE ARE MY BASIC YARDAGES:

DRIVER	250 UP
3-WOOD	235 UP
1-IRON	215 - 235
2-IRON	205 - 220
3-IRON	195 - 210
4-IRON	185 - 200
5-IRON	170 - 185
6-IRON	155 - 170
7-IRON	140 - 155
8-IRON	130 - 145
9-IRON	105 - 135
PITCHING WEDGE	80 - 130
SAND WEDGE	UP TO 100

STEP OFF YOURS.
AND WHEN IN DOUBT,
TAKE MORE CLUB
AND
SWING SMOOTHLY.

Figure Distances Carefully

OBJECTS THAT OFFER SIZE AND PERSPECTIVE COMPARISON WILL HELP YOU JUDGE DISTANCES BETTER ON STRANGE COURSES. TREES, BUNKERS, PLAYERS ON THE GREEN, THE HEIGHT OF THE PIN ARE ALL USEFUL AIDS.

JM

10 YDS 10 YDS 10 YDS

WEDGE DISTANCE

BETTER YET IS THE "PROGRESSION" METHOD. SIGHT AN OBJECT THAT IS SAY WEDGE-SHOT DISTANCE AHEAD OF YOUR BALL, THEN ESTIMATE FROM THERE TO THE PIN IN 10-YARD INCREMENTS. EACH INCREMENT EQUALS ONE MORE CLUB. ABOVE ALL, **BE UP**.

IF YOU'RE STILL IN DOUBT, TAKE ONE MORE CLUB THAN YOU FIGURED AND SWING SMOOTHLY.

STATISTICS PROVE THAT TOUR PROS GENERALLY DRIVE THE BALL SHORTER THAN MANY FANS IMAGINE THEY DO — ONLY ABOUT 250 YARDS ON AVERAGE.

WATCHING PRO-AM PARTNERS PROVES TO ME THAT MOST HANDICAP GOLFERS ALSO DRIVE THE BALL SHORTER THAN THEY THINK THEY DO — WHICH IS ONE REASON THEY'RE SO CONSISTENTLY SHORT ON SECOND SHOTS. SO BE REALISTIC — USE ENOUGH CLUB.

5-IRON

NOPE... THIS 6 WILL DO IT...

Consider Putts When Planning Approaches

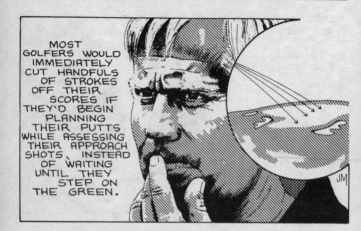

MOST GOLFERS WOULD IMMEDIATELY CUT HANDFULS OF STROKES OFF THEIR SCORES IF THEY'D BEGIN PLANNING THEIR PUTTS WHILE ASSESSING THEIR APPROACH SHOTS, INSTEAD OF WAITING UNTIL THEY STEP ON THE GREEN.

JM

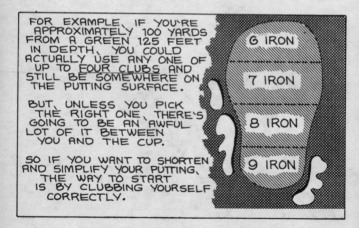

FOR EXAMPLE, IF YOU'RE APPROXIMATELY 100 YARDS FROM A GREEN 125 FEET IN DEPTH, YOU COULD ACTUALLY USE ANY ONE OF UP TO FOUR CLUBS AND STILL BE SOMEWHERE ON THE PUTTING SURFACE.

BUT, UNLESS YOU PICK THE RIGHT ONE, THERE'S GOING TO BE AN AWFUL LOT OF IT BETWEEN YOU AND THE CUP.

SO IF YOU WANT TO SHORTEN AND SIMPLIFY YOUR PUTTING, THE WAY TO START IS BY CLUBBING YOURSELF CORRECTLY.

6 IRON

7 IRON

8 IRON

9 IRON

Give Yourself Margin for Error

AT BEST, I HIT ONLY FOUR OR FIVE SHOTS A ROUND EXACTLY AS I'VE PLANNED THEM MENTALLY. FOR THAT REASON, I TRY TO LEAVE MYSELF SOME MARGIN FOR ERROR ON ALL APPROACHES.

WITH THE PIN ON THE RIGHT, FOR EXAMPLE, I'LL AIM FOR THE GREEN CENTER AND ATTEMPT TO FADE THE BALL TO THE HOLE. WITH THE PIN ON THE LEFT, I REVERSE THE PROCEDURE BY TRYING TO DRAW THE BALL IN. THIS WAY, I'LL GEN-ERALLY BE PUTTING EVEN IF I DON'T FADE OR DRAW AS MUCH AS PLANNED.

Know When Not to Attack

KNOWING WHERE **NOT** TO ATTACK IN GOLF IS AS CRITICAL AS KNOWING WHEN TO PLAY BOLDLY.

NO. 11 AT **A**UGUSTA **N**ATIONAL IS A GOOD EXAMPLE.

THERE IS A STRONG RISK HERE OF A LONG SECOND EITHER FALLING SHORT OR KICKING AND ROLLING INTO THE WATER IMMEDIATELY FRONTING THE GREEN.

THUS I ALMOST ALWAYS PLAY THE HOLE AS A "PAR 4½," APPROACHING TO THE **RIGHT SIDE** OF THE GREEN AND RELYING ON A CHIP OR LONG PUTT TO GET MY PAR.

JM

Keep an Eye on Upcoming Holes

YOU CAN SAVE A LOT OF SHOTS ON DOG-LEG HOLES BY KNOWING THE PIN POSITION IN ADVANCE.

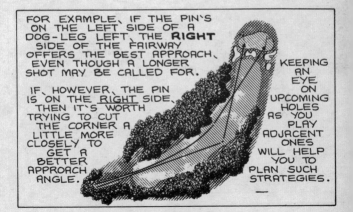

FOR EXAMPLE, IF THE PIN'S ON THE LEFT SIDE OF A DOG-LEG LEFT, THE **RIGHT** SIDE OF THE FAIRWAY OFFERS THE BEST APPROACH, EVEN THOUGH A LONGER SHOT MAY BE CALLED FOR.

IF, HOWEVER, THE PIN IS ON THE RIGHT SIDE, THEN IT'S WORTH TRYING TO CUT THE CORNER A LITTLE MORE CLOSELY TO GET A BETTER APPROACH ANGLE.

KEEPING AN EYE ON UPCOMING HOLES AS YOU PLAY ADJACENT ONES WILL HELP YOU TO PLAN SUCH STRATEGIES.
—

PLAYERS WHO SET THE BALL UP ON GRASSY TUFTS AT EVERY OPPORTUNITY SHOW LACK OF GOLFING SOPHISTICATION AS WELL AS LACK OF CONFIDENCE.

WHAT THEY'RE DOING IS CREATING EXACTLY THE SITUATION THAT ALL FINE PLAYERS HATE AND AVOID — THE "FLIER LIE."

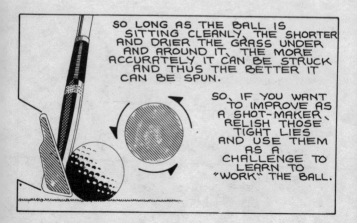

SO LONG AS THE BALL IS SITTING CLEANLY, THE SHORTER AND DRIER THE GRASS UNDER AND AROUND IT, THE MORE ACCURATELY IT CAN BE STRUCK AND THUS THE BETTER IT CAN BE SPUN.

SO, IF YOU WANT TO IMPROVE AS A SHOT-MAKER, RELISH THOSE TIGHT LIES AND USE THEM AS A CHALLENGE TO LEARN TO "WORK" THE BALL.

Bear This Clubbing Factor in Mind

HERE'S A PIECE OF INFORMATION THAT CAN IMPROVE YOUR CLUB SELECTION, ESPECIALLY IN WIND: THE LESS LOFTED THE CLUB, THE MORE CONTROL YOU HAVE OVER ITS **STARTING** DIRECTION.

THEREFORE, UNLESS YOU TEND TO SLICE OR HOOK THE BALL BADLY, IT OFTEN PAYS TO GO WITH THE **LEAST-LOFTED** CLUB WHENEVER YOU ARE IN DOUBT ABOUT AN APPROACH SHOT. USE THIS STRATEGY PARTICULARLY IN WIND: FOR INSTANCE, PLAY A THREE-QUARTER 9-IRON INSTEAD OF A FULL WEDGE INTO HEAD OR CROSS-WINDS.

Restrict Long-Irons to Good Lies

IF YOU HAVE DIFFICULTY WITH THE LONG IRONS — AND MOST HIGH HANDICAPPERS DO — THEN MAKE IT A RULE NEVER TO PLAY THEM FROM A POOR OR "TIGHT" LIE. USE A FAIRWAY WOOD INSTEAD.

3-IRON, PLEASE.... NO, LET'S GO WITH THE 5-WOOD!

JM

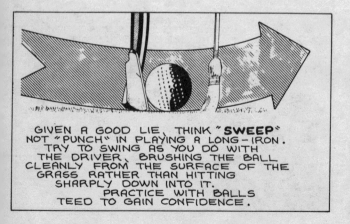

GIVEN A GOOD LIE, THINK **"SWEEP"** NOT "PUNCH" IN PLAYING A LONG-IRON. TRY TO SWING AS YOU DO WITH THE DRIVER, BRUSHING THE BALL CLEANLY FROM THE SURFACE OF THE GRASS RATHER THAN HITTING SHARPLY DOWN INTO IT. PRACTICE WITH BALLS TEED TO GAIN CONFIDENCE.

WHEN INDECISIVE ABOUT SACRIFICING DISTANCE FOR ACCURACY, ASK YOURSELF THIS: "IS THE POSSIBLE REWARD FOR ADDED DISTANCE WORTH THE RISK I MUST TAKE TO GET IT?"

REMEMBER, PLAYING A WEDGE TO THE GREEN WOULD BE WONDERFUL, BUT A 7-IRON APPROACH FROM SHORT GRASS IS BETTER THAN CHIPPING OUT OF THE FOREST OR BLASTING A FEW YARDS OUT OF A FAIRWAY BUNKER.

PUT COMMON SENSE AHEAD OF PRIDE AND PLAY FOR <u>POSITION</u>.

11

In the Wind and Wet

Be Patient, Keep Control

EVER NOTICED THAT THE BEST PLAYERS ALMOST ALWAYS COME TO THE TOP WHEN THE WIND BLOWS HARD?

ONE REASON IS THEIR TECHNICAL SHOT-MAKING ABILITY. BUT THERE'S MORE TO IT THAN THAT.

THE INTELLIGENT GOLFER RECOGNIZES WIND AS ONE OF THE GAME'S TOUGHEST CHALLENGES, WHICH CAUSES HIM TO BE **MORE PATIENT** AND EXERCISE EVEN **GREATER SELF-CONTROL** THAN NORMAL.

THE LESS SAVVY PLAYER LETS WIND MAKE HIM ANGRY AND FEARFUL, WHICH EMOTIONS ARE RAPIDLY REFLECTED IN HIS SOARING SCORES.

DO YOU LIKE TO TEST WIND STRENGTH AND DIRECTION BY TOSSING GRASS IN THE AIR?

THAT DEFINITELY CAN HELP IN PROVIDING INFORMATION. BUT SOMETIMES IT DOESN'T PROVIDE ENOUGH FOR MY LIKING.

WHAT'S HAPPENING NEAR GROUND-LEVEL ISN'T NECESSARILY WHAT'S HAPPENING UP WHERE THE BALL IS GOING. FOR THAT REASON, I'LL GENERALLY LOOK UP HIGH AT WHAT'S HAPPENING TO THE TREE-TOPS WHENEVER THE WIND BLOWS HARD.

TRY THIS IF YOU FREQUENTLY MIS-READ WIND STRENGTH OR DIRECTION.

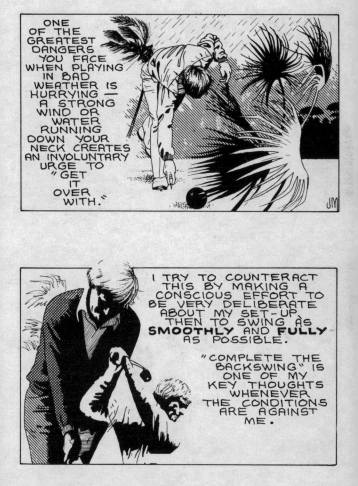

ONE OF THE GREATEST DANGERS YOU FACE WHEN PLAYING IN BAD WEATHER IS HURRYING — A STRONG WIND OR WATER RUNNING DOWN YOUR NECK CREATES AN INVOLUNTARY URGE TO "GET IT OVER WITH."

I TRY TO COUNTERACT THIS BY MAKING A CONSCIOUS EFFORT TO BE VERY DELIBERATE ABOUT MY SET-UP, THEN TO SWING AS **SMOOTHLY** AND **FULLY** AS POSSIBLE.

"COMPLETE THE BACKSWING" IS ONE OF MY KEY THOUGHTS WHENEVER THE CONDITIONS ARE AGAINST ME.

Don't Tee Lower into the Wind

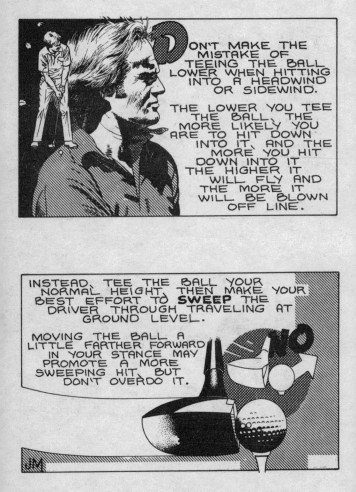

DON'T MAKE THE MISTAKE OF TEEING THE BALL LOWER WHEN HITTING INTO A HEADWIND OR SIDEWIND.

THE LOWER YOU TEE THE BALL, THE MORE LIKELY YOU ARE TO HIT DOWN INTO IT, AND THE MORE YOU HIT DOWN INTO IT THE HIGHER IT WILL FLY AND THE MORE IT WILL BE BLOWN OFF LINE.

INSTEAD, TEE THE BALL YOUR NORMAL HEIGHT, THEN MAKE YOUR BEST EFFORT TO **SWEEP** THE DRIVER THROUGH TRAVELING AT GROUND LEVEL.

MOVING THE BALL A LITTLE FARTHER FORWARD IN YOUR STANCE MAY PROMOTE A MORE SWEEPING HIT, BUT DON'T OVERDO IT.

NO

Swing Easier with More Club

BIG PROBLEM WHEN PLAYING INTO A STRONG HEADWIND IS THE RISK OF "BALLOONING" SHOTS. FREQUENTLY THE BALL'S TENDENCY TO SOAR IS INCREASED BY THE EXTRA BACKSPIN IMPARTED BY YOUR NATURAL TENDENCY TO HIT IT HARDER.

I GENERALLY ATTEMPT TO COUNTER BOTH TENDENCIES BY HITTING _EASIER_ RATHER THAN HARDER. IF THE SHOT NORMALLY WOULD CALL FOR SAY A G-IRON, I'LL TAKE A 4-IRON AND SWING _SOFTLY_. THIS IMPARTS LESS BACKSPIN, WHICH KEEPS THE BALL LOWER AND THUS MAKES IT BORE BETTER THROUGH THE WIND.

Consider Wind's Stopping Effect

REMEMBER THAT, INTO A HEADWIND, LESS LOFT GENERALLY MEANS GREATER CONTROL. SO, IF THE SHOT NORMALLY WOULD CALL FOR A WEDGE, CONSIDER USING THE NINE-IRON INSTEAD.

IF UNDER STILL CONDITIONS YOU'D HIT A THREE-QUARTER WEDGE, MAKE A HALF-SWING WITH THE NINE-IRON. IF THE WIND IS EXTREMELY STRONG, CONSIDER EVEN GOING TO THE EIGHT-IRON. REMEMBER THAT, THE STRONGER THE WIND, THE GREATER ITS STOPPING EFFECT ON THE BALL, EVEN THOUGH YOU HIT IT LOW.

Swing More Compact for Better Balance

BALANCE IS A CRITICAL FACTOR ON ALL GOLF SHOTS. BUT SOMETIMES — SUCH AS IN WINDY OR WET WEATHER — IT'S VERY DIFFICULT TO ACHIEVE USING YOUR NORMAL SWING. IN THOSE INSTANCES, CONSIDER COMPACTING YOUR SWING.

JM

MY WAY IS GENERALLY TO USE LESS BODY MOTION AND MORE HAND ACTION. THE CHIEF ADJUSTMENT IS TO RELAX MY WRISTS MORE GOING BACK, WHICH ALLOWS THEM TO COCK EARLIER AND MORE FULLY. THIS IN TURN CREATES A MATCHING LIVELINESS OF WRIST ACTION THROUGH IMPACT, CREATING GOOD CLUBHEAD SPEED WITHOUT A GREAT DEAL OF BODY MOVEMENT.

Adjust Like This for Wider Stance

A WIDER STANCE WILL GIVE YOU BETTER ANCHORAGE AND BALANCE WHEN PLAYING IN A STRONG WIND, BUT IT ALSO CREATES A RESTRICTION THAT NEEDS TO BE COMPENSATED FOR.

WIDENING THE STANCE SHORTENS THE BACKSWING BY REDUCING BODY TURN, WHICH GENERALLY REDUCES DISTANCE. THE ANSWER IS TO TAKE AT LEAST <u>ONE MORE CLUB</u> THAN NORMAL — WHICH ALSO HAS THE ADDITIONAL BENEFIT OF FLYING THE BALL LOWER.

Try These Approaches Downwind

THERE ARE TWO WAYS TO PLAY A DOWNWIND APPROACH. THE SAFEST AND EASIEST WAY, WHEN THERE ARE NO FRONTAL HAZARDS, IS TO LAND THE BALL SHORT AND LET IT ROLL ONTO THE GREEN.

WITH TROUBLE IN FRONT OF THE GREEN, A HIGH, SOFT-LANDING SHOT IS NECESSARY. YOU CAN INCREASE STOPPING POWER BY FADING THE BALL IN WHEN THE GREEN SLOPES TO THE LEFT, AND DRAWING IT WHEN THE GREEN SLOPES TO THE RIGHT.

Accept the Extra Challenge

THERE ARE THREE WAYS TO APPROACH WET WEATHER GOLF.

ONE IS TO STAY HOME UNTIL CONDITIONS DRY UP, AND THE SECOND IS TO PLAY BUT WITH A NEGATIVE ATTITUDE AND A LOT OF GRIPING — AND, INVARIABLY, POOR SCORES.

THE THIRD WAY, WHICH I FAVOR, IS TO ACCEPT THE RAIN AS JUST ANOTHER OF THE GAME'S MANY CHALLENGES AND ENJOY MEETING IT AS BEST YOU CAN. HOWEVER, RECOGNIZING THAT YOU AREN'T LIKELY TO SHOOT YOUR RECORD SCORE IS CRITICAL TO PLAYING INTELLIGENT SHOTS UNDER SUCH CONDITIONS.

WATCH THE P G A TOUR AND YOU'LL NOTICE HOW METICULOUS ALL THE PLAYERS ARE ABOUT CLEANING OFF THEIR GOLF SHOE SPIKES, ESPECIALLY IN WET OR SLOPPY CONDITIONS.

THEY DO SO TO AVOID THE DISASTER SHOTS THAT CAN COME FROM SLIPPING DURING THE SWING, AND SO SHOULD YOU. SIMPLY TAKE A TEE OR PITCH - MARK REPAIRER AND SCRAPE OUT ANY GOOK BEFORE ALL FULL SHOTS.

Drive for Maximum Carry

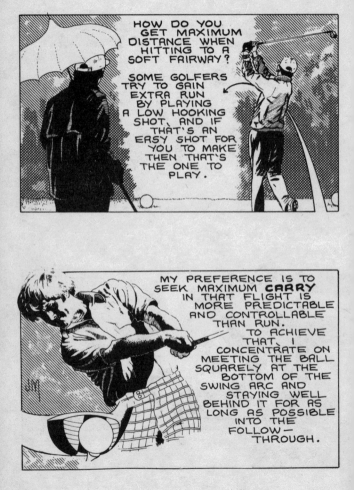

HOW DO YOU GET MAXIMUM DISTANCE WHEN HITTING TO A SOFT FAIRWAY?

SOME GOLFERS TRY TO GAIN EXTRA RUN BY PLAYING A LOW HOOKING SHOT, AND IF THAT'S AN EASY SHOT FOR YOU TO MAKE THEN THAT'S THE ONE TO PLAY.

MY PREFERENCE IS TO SEEK MAXIMUM **CARRY** IN THAT FLIGHT IS MORE PREDICTABLE AND CONTROLLABLE THAN RUN. TO ACHIEVE THAT, I CONCENTRATE ON MEETING THE BALL SQUARELY AT THE BOTTOM OF THE SWING ARC AND STAYING WELL BEHIND IT FOR AS LONG AS POSSIBLE INTO THE FOLLOW-THROUGH.

Don't Be Too Fancy

NEVER TRY TO BE TOO FANCY WITH THE LONGER CLUBS OFF WET TURF OR WHEN PLAYING IN RAIN.

WHEN WATER COMES BETWEEN THE CLUBFACE AND THE BALL IT DIMINISHES SIDESPIN, AS WELL AS HEIGHT.

THUS AN ATTEMPTED FADE WILL OFTEN FLY PRETTY MUCH STRAIGHT LEFT IN WET CONDITIONS, AND AN ATTEMPTED DRAW STRAIGHT RIGHT. BEST POLICY IS A STRAIGHT SHOT, WITH AS AMPLY LOFTED A CLUB AS POSSIBLE RELATIVE TO THE DISTANCE TO BE COVERED.

12

Getting Out of Trouble

TASK NO. 1,
WHENEVER YOU STRAY
FROM THE
SHORT GRASS, IS:
STAY COOL.

THE MORE YOU
LET ANGER OR
FEAR INFLUENCE
YOUR ACTIONS,
THE GREATER
YOUR CHANCE
OF COMPOUNDING
THE ERROR
INTO A
DISASTER.

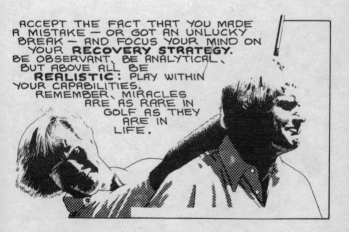

ACCEPT THE FACT THAT YOU MADE
A MISTAKE — OR GOT AN UNLUCKY
BREAK — AND FOCUS YOUR MIND ON
YOUR **RECOVERY STRATEGY.**
BE OBSERVANT, BE ANALYTICAL,
BUT ABOVE ALL BE
REALISTIC: PLAY WITHIN
YOUR CAPABILITIES.
REMEMBER, MIRACLES
ARE AS RARE IN
GOLF AS THEY
ARE IN
LIFE.

Take Less Club for "Flier" Lie

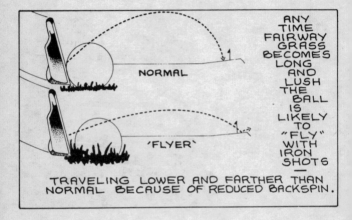

ANY TIME FAIRWAY GRASS BECOMES LONG AND LUSH THE BALL IS LIKELY TO "FLY" WITH IRON SHOTS — TRAVELING LOWER AND FARTHER THAN NORMAL BECAUSE OF REDUCED BACKSPIN.

I COUNTERACT THAT BY GOING DOWN A CLUB — SAY FROM A SIX- TO A SEVEN-IRON — WHICH AUTOMATICALLY PRODUCES LESS DISTANCE.

THEN, TO GAIN MAXIMUM HEIGHT, I MOVE THE BALL A LITTLE FORWARD AT ADDRESS AND MAKE SURE I **RELEASE** FULLY WITH THE WRISTS GOING THROUGH.

Know This Key Rule in Rough

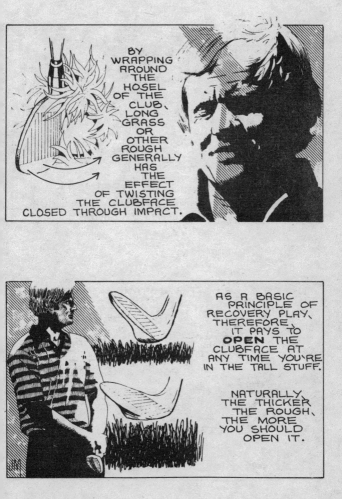

BY WRAPPING AROUND THE HOSEL OF THE CLUB, LONG GRASS OR OTHER ROUGH GENERALLY HAS THE EFFECT OF TWISTING THE CLUBFACE CLOSED THROUGH IMPACT.

AS A BASIC PRINCIPLE OF RECOVERY PLAY, THEREFORE, IT PAYS TO **OPEN** THE CLUBFACE AT ANY TIME YOU'RE IN THE TALL STUFF.

NATURALLY THE THICKER THE ROUGH, THE MORE YOU SHOULD OPEN IT.

Fit Shot to Grass Direction

IN ROUGH, THE DIRECTION OF GRASS GROWTH WILL OFTEN AFFECT THE BEHAVIOR OF THE BALL. FOR INSTANCE, WHEN THE GRASS LIES **AGAINST** THE SHOT IT WILL TEND TO CHECK AND CLOSE THE CLUBFACE MORE THAN USUAL, SO CLUB YOURSELF AND AIM ACCORDINGLY.

THERE'S LESS RESISTANCE WHEN THE GRASS LIES **TOWARDS** THE TARGET, BUT THE BALL WILL OFTEN TEND TO "FLY" BECAUSE OF REDUCED BACKSPIN. THEREFORE, FROM THIS TYPE OF LIE IT GENERALLY PAYS TO TAKE LESS CLUB THAN NORMAL, AND TO ALLOW FOR EXTRA RUN.

I PLAY BASICALLY TWO TYPES OF SHOT FROM ROUGH.

HERE'S MY TECHNIQUE WHEN NEEDING A HIGH-FLYING, SOFT-LANDING SHOT WITH AS MUCH SPIN AS I CAN GENERATE DESPITE GRASS GETTING BETWEEN THE CLUBFACE AND BALL AT IMPACT.

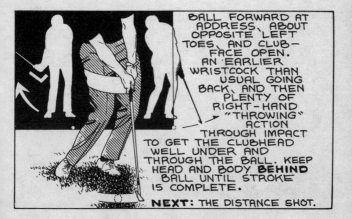

BALL FORWARD AT ADDRESS, ABOUT OPPOSITE LEFT TOES, AND CLUBFACE OPEN. AN EARLIER WRISTCOCK THAN USUAL GOING BACK, AND THEN PLENTY OF RIGHT-HAND "THROWING" ACTION THROUGH IMPACT TO GET THE CLUBHEAD WELL UNDER AND THROUGH THE BALL. KEEP HEAD AND BODY **BEHIND** BALL UNTIL STROKE IS COMPLETE.

NEXT: THE DISTANCE SHOT.

SO LONG AS YOU DON'T HAVE TO FLY THE BALL HIGH OR LAND IT SOFTLY, THERE'S A WAY TO GET DISTANCE FROM HEAVY, GRASSY LIES.

TAKE A CLUB OR TWO LESS THAN YOU'D NORMALLY PLAY, MOVE THE BALL WELL BACK IN YOUR STANCE, THEN HIT STEEPLY DOWN ONTO IT WITH A <u>HARD</u>, <u>PUNCHING</u> DELIVERY.

IT'S A FAIRLY UNCONTROLLED AND CERTAINLY AN INELEGANT SHOT, BUT PLAYED CORRECTLY IT WILL SQUIRT THE BALL OUT LOW AND WITH LOTS OF RUN.

Aim Off for Angled Lies

WHEN THE BALL IS BELOW YOUR FEET YOU'LL TEND TO SWING MORE UPRIGHT, WHICH MAY PRODUCE A FADE OR SLICE. WHEN THE BALL IS ABOVE YOUR FEET YOU'LL NORMALLY SWING FLATTER, WHICH USUALLY CREATES A DRAW OR HOOK.

JM

EASIEST WAY TO COUNTERACT THIS IS SIMPLY TO AIM OFF AT ADDRESS TO ALLOW FOR THE CURVE — TO THE **LEFT** WHEN THE BALL IS BELOW YOUR FEET, AND TO THE **RIGHT** WHEN IT'S ABOVE. REMEMBER, HOWEVER, THAT THE MORE ANGLED THE LIE THE MORE SUCH SHOTS WILL CURVE, SO ALLOW ACCORDINGLY.

Bear Down When "Divotted"

DON'T GIVE UP WHEN YOUR BALL LANDS IN A DIVOT HOLE.

THERE ARE TWO WAYS TO BEAT THIS UNLUCKY BREAK. FIRST, IF YOU CAN RUN THE BALL ONTO THE GREEN, PLAY A PUNCH SHOT — BALL BACK, HANDS AHEAD AT ADDRESS AND IMPACT, THREE-QUARTER SWING, FIRM HIT.

IF YOU MUST FLY THE BALL TO THE TARGET, MOVE THE BALL FORWARD, OPEN THE CLUBFACE, SWING FULLY, AND HIT HARD WITH THE RIGHT HAND **WITHOUT ALLOWING IT TO ROLL OVER THE LEFT** UNTIL WELL AFTER IMPACT. ALLOW FOR A FADE — AND, IN BOTH CASES, KEEP YOUR HEAD STILL.

Use Woods to "Dig" for Distance

GETTING DISTANCE FROM A DIVOT MARK, OR OTHER SHALLOW DEPRESSION, IS MUCH EASIER WITH THE FAIRWAY WOODS THAN THE LONG IRONS FOR MOST PLAYERS.

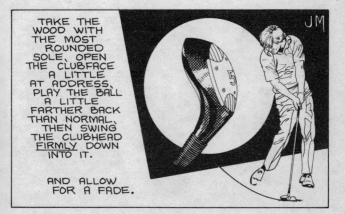

TAKE THE WOOD WITH THE MOST ROUNDED SOLE, OPEN THE CLUBFACE A LITTLE AT ADDRESS, PLAY THE BALL A LITTLE FARTHER BACK THAN NORMAL, THEN SWING THE CLUBHEAD FIRMLY DOWN INTO IT.

AND ALLOW FOR A FADE.

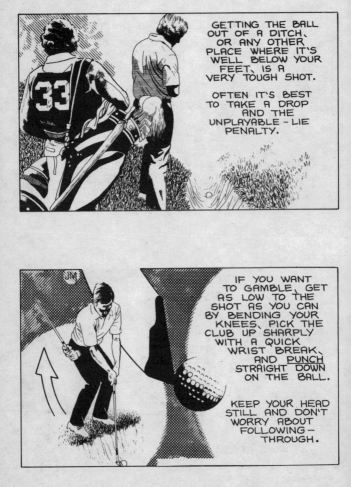

GETTING THE BALL OUT OF A DITCH, OR ANY OTHER PLACE WHERE IT'S WELL BELOW YOUR FEET, IS A VERY TOUGH SHOT.

OFTEN IT'S BEST TO TAKE A DROP AND THE UNPLAYABLE-LIE PENALTY.

IF YOU WANT TO GAMBLE, GET AS LOW TO THE SHOT AS YOU CAN BY BENDING YOUR KNEES, PICK THE CLUB UP SHARPLY WITH A QUICK WRIST BREAK, AND PUNCH STRAIGHT DOWN ON THE BALL.

KEEP YOUR HEAD STILL AND DON'T WORRY ABOUT FOLLOWING-THROUGH.

Let Club Loft Lift ball from Hard-Pan

THERE'S ONE <u>ABSOLUTE</u> RULE WHENEVER YOU ARE OBLIGED TO HIT FROM ANY FORM OF HARDPAN.

THAT IS TO ALLOW THE **LOFT OF THE CLUB** TO LIFT THE BALL, RATHER THAN TRYING TO DO IT WITH YOUR SWING.

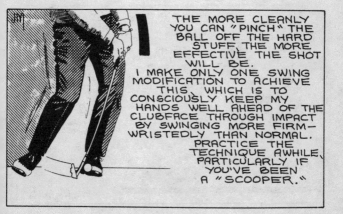

THE MORE CLEANLY YOU CAN "PINCH" THE BALL OFF THE HARD STUFF, THE MORE EFFECTIVE THE SHOT WILL BE.
I MAKE ONLY ONE SWING MODIFICATION TO ACHIEVE THIS, WHICH IS TO CONSCIOUSLY KEEP MY HANDS WELL AHEAD OF THE CLUBFACE THROUGH IMPACT BY SWINGING MORE FIRM-WRISTEDLY THAN NORMAL. PRACTICE THE TECHNIQUE AWHILE, PARTICULARLY IF YOU'VE BEEN A "SCOOPER."

Use Sand-Shot Technique from Water

WHAT SHOULD YOU DO WHEN THE BALL IS IN WATER BUT STILL VISIBLE AND REACHABLE?

IF IT'S TOTALLY SUBMERGED, MY ADVICE IS DROP CLEAR AND TAKE YOUR PENALTY. BECAUSE THE CHANCES OF A DECENT RECOVERY ARE DEFINITELY AGAINST YOU.

JM

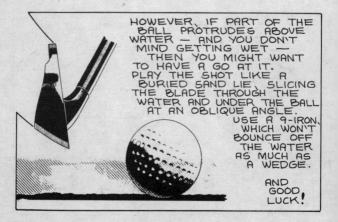

HOWEVER, IF PART OF THE BALL PROTRUDES ABOVE WATER — AND YOU DON'T MIND GETTING WET — THEN YOU MIGHT WANT TO HAVE A GO AT IT. PLAY THE SHOT LIKE A BURIED SAND LIE, SLICING THE BLADE THROUGH THE WATER AND UNDER THE BALL AT AN OBLIQUE ANGLE.

USE A 9-IRON, WHICH WON'T BOUNCE OFF THE WATER AS MUCH AS A WEDGE.

AND GOOD LUCK!

Release *Fully* to Clear Tree-Tops

HITTING OVER TREES IS LESS OF A PROBLEM THAN MOST AMATEURS BELIEVE IT TO BE, GIVEN THE MINOR SWING MODIFICATIONS THAT PRODUCE HIGHER-FLYING SHOTS.

OPEN THE CLUBFACE SLIGHTLY AND ALLOW FOR A FADE. COMING DOWN, KEEP YOUR HEAD WELL BEHIND THE BALL AND BE SURE TO GET WELL UNDER IT BY RELEASING YOUR WRISTS A LITTLE EARLIER THAN USUAL.

FOR EVEN GREATER HEIGHT, MOVE THE BALL FARTHER FORWARD IN YOUR STANCE.

Concentrate on Swing, Not Lie

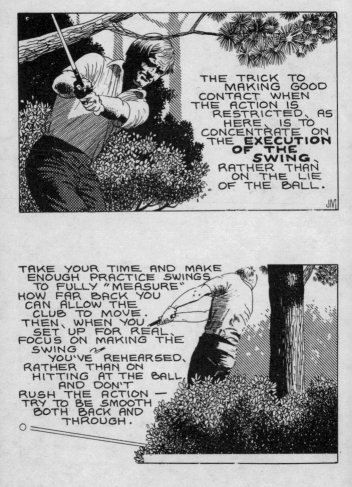

THE TRICK TO MAKING GOOD CONTACT WHEN THE ACTION IS RESTRICTED, AS HERE, IS TO CONCENTRATE ON THE **EXECUTION OF THE SWING,** RATHER THAN ON THE LIE OF THE BALL.

JM

TAKE YOUR TIME AND MAKE ENOUGH PRACTICE SWINGS TO FULLY "MEASURE" HOW FAR BACK YOU CAN ALLOW THE CLUB TO MOVE. THEN, WHEN YOU SET UP FOR REAL, FOCUS ON MAKING THE SWING YOU'VE REHEARSED, RATHER THAN ON HITTING AT THE BALL, AND DON'T RUSH THE ACTION — TRY TO BE SMOOTH BOTH BACK AND THROUGH.

Don't Risk a Penalty Here

IT'S EASY TO INCUR A PENALTY BY CAUSING THE BALL TO MOVE WHEN IT'S SITTING ON LOOSE MATERIALS, LIKE LEAVES OR PINE NEEDLES.

TO MINIMIZE THAT RISK I AVOID GROUNDING THE CLUB AT ADDRESS.

BECAUSE THE BALL CAN'T BE "GRIPPED" AS CLEANLY ON THE CLUBFACE, IT WILL USUALLY FLY LOWER AND RUN FARTHER FROM SUCH A LIE.

ALLOW FOR THAT IN ASSESSING THE SHOT.

"Explode" Ball from "Straw" Lie

LOTS OF PINE NEEDLES WHERE YOU PLAY?

HERE'S A WAY TO PITCH THE BALL OUT OF A "STRAW" LIE THAT IS PARTICULARLY USEFUL WHEN YOU MUST GET IT UP FAST.

PLAY A BUNKER-TYPE **EXPLOSION** SHOT. USING A SAND- OR PITCHING-WEDGE, PICK THE CLUB UP QUICKLY WITH AN OPEN FACE, AND HIT DOWN AND THROUGH ABOUT AN INCH BEHIND THE BALL.

SWING A LITTLE HARDER THAN YOU WOULD FOR THE SAME DISTANCE FROM GRASS.

Meet Ball before Sand

A FUNDAMENTAL OF ACHIEVING DISTANCE FROM BUNKERS IS MEETING THE BALL BEFORE THE CLUBHEAD CATCHES THE SAND.

MOVING THE HANDS FORWARD AND/OR THE BALL BACK AT ADDRESS FACILITATES THIS CLEAN "PICKING" ACTION.

JM

HOWEVER, BOTH THESE SET-UP ADJUSTMENTS ALSO HAVE THE EFFECT OF <u>REDUCING</u> EFFECTIVE CLUBFACE LOFT. SO CONSIDER TAKING A MORE LOFTED CLUB THAN YOU NORMALLY WOULD ANY TIME YOU HAVE A HIGH LIP AHEAD OF YOU.

YOU WON'T ALWAYS REACH THE GREEN FROM A FAIRWAY BUNKER, BUT YOU CAN OFTEN GET CLOSE ENOUGH TO IT TO SALVAGE PAR IF YOU HAVE DEVELOPED A BASIC "ESCAPE" SHOT.

6-IRON

4-IRON

ABSOLUTE **MUST** IS TO CHOOSE A CLUB THAT WILL ENABLE YOU TO EASILY CLEAR THE FRONT LIP. AFTER THAT, CHOKE DOWN ON THE CLUB A LITTLE (TO MAKE UP FOR YOUR FEET HAVING WRIGGLED DOWN INTO THE SAND), LOOK AND AIM AT THE TOP OF THE BALL, AND SWING **FREELY**.

ATTEMPT THIS SHOT ONLY FROM A GOOD LIE.

JM

Consider the "Long Explosion"...

DON'T GIVE UP ON REACH-ING THE GREEN IF YOU'RE FACED WITH A POOR LIE IN A FAIRWAY BUNKER WITHIN NORMAL SHORT-IRON RANGE OF THE GREEN. TRY A LONG EXPLOSION SHOT.

TAKE TWO CLUBS MORE THAN THE DISTANCE WOULD NORMALLY REQUIRE, PLANT YOURSELF FIRMLY, OPEN THE CLUBFACE WIDE, AIM LEFT TO ALLOW FOR THE INEVITABLE FADE, MAKE A FULL SWING, AND HIT HARD INTO THE SAND AS CLOSE TO THE BALL AS YOU CAN.

THIS IS A VALUABLE RECOVERY SHOT TECHNIQUE, BUT IT NEEDS PRACTICE TO BE PLAYED CONFIDENTLY.

...and the "Cut Blast"

IF CIRCUMSTANCES DEMAND THAT YOU **MUST** GO FOR DISTANCE FROM A "FLUFFY" BUNKER LIE, TRY HITTING A **CUT BLAST SHOT** WITH A ROUND-SOLED FOUR- OR FIVE-WOOD.

THE HEAVY, ROUNDED SOLE OF THE WOOD GIVES YOU A BETTER CHANCE OF BLASTING THROUGH INTERVENING SAND THAN A LIGHT-HEADED, STRAIGHT-SOLED MEDIUM- OR LONG-IRON. CUTTING ACROSS THE SHOT A LITTLE FROM OUT TO IN REDUCES THE AMOUNT OF SAND YOU TAKE BY STEEPENING YOUR SWING ARC.

Play Normal Bunker Shot from Sand-spill

A BALL LAYING ON SAND SPILL NEAR THE EDGE OF A BUNKER IS EASIER TO PLAY THAN IT LOOKS.

NORMALLY FROM SAND THE DEPTH OF CUT IS CRITICAL TO PROVIDING THE CLUBHEAD BOUNCE NECESSARY TO GET BENEATH THE BALL. BUT IN THIS SITUATION THE GROUND BELOW THE LIGHT SAND LAYER IS A NICE INSURANCE AGAINST DIGGING TOO DEEPLY.

SO GO AHEAD AND USE YOUR SAND-WEDGE AND JUST PLAY THE SHOT AS YOU WOULD FROM A NORMAL GREENSIDE BUNKER LIE, HITTING A COUPLE OF INCHES BEHIND THE BALL AND MAKING SURE TO FOLLOW-THROUGH.

THERE ARE MANY SITUATIONS IN GOLF THAT PROHIBIT A HIGH PITCH:
1) A VERY TIGHT LIE,
2) A MOUND GUARDING A TIGHT PIN PLACEMENT,
3) OVERHANGING LIMBS, ETC.

SUCH CHALLENGES CALL FOR A LOW BOUNCE-AND-RUN SHOT WITH A LONG-IRON. POSITION THE BALL BACK NEAR YOUR RIGHT FOOT WITH YOUR HANDS WELL FORWARD OF IT, THEN HIT CRISPLY DOWN INTO ITS BACK WITH A SHORT, FIRM SWING.

PRACTICE THE SHOT TO GET A FEEL FOR HOW FAR THE BALL WILL RUN.

Be Firm on *This* Tough Pitch

IMPARTING HEAVY BACKSPIN TO A PITCH SHOT FROM ROUGH ISN'T EASY, BUT IT CAN BE DONE IF THE LIE IS NOT TOO TERRIBLE.

TRICK IS TO OPEN THE CLUBFACE AT ADDRESS, THEN PICK THE CLUB UP WITH THE WRISTS VERY ABRUPTLY AND HIT <u>SHARPLY DOWN</u> INTO THE BALL.

THE STEEPER THE ANGLE OF ATTACK, THE BETTER YOUR CHANCE OF GETTING BALL BEFORE GRASS.

BUT THIS IS A SHOT WHERE YOU REALLY DO HAVE TO STRIKE **FIRMLY** — AND <u>LOOK AT THE BALL.</u> WHILE DOING SO.

Use Your Imagination

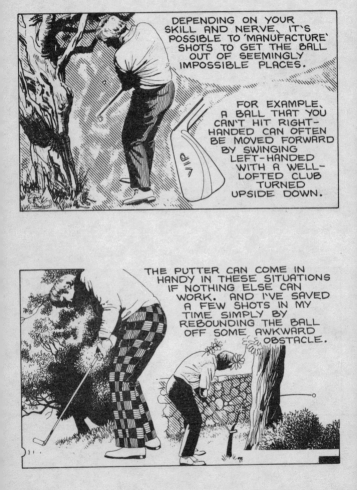

DEPENDING ON YOUR SKILL AND NERVE, IT'S POSSIBLE TO 'MANUFACTURE' SHOTS TO GET THE BALL OUT OF SEEMINGLY IMPOSSIBLE PLACES.

FOR EXAMPLE, A BALL THAT YOU CAN'T HIT RIGHT-HANDED CAN OFTEN BE MOVED FORWARD BY SWINGING LEFT-HANDED WITH A WELL-LOFTED CLUB TURNED UPSIDE DOWN.

THE PUTTER CAN COME IN HANDY IN THESE SITUATIONS IF NOTHING ELSE CAN WORK. AND I'VE SAVED A FEW SHOTS IN MY TIME SIMPLY BY REBOUNDING THE BALL OFF SOME AWKWARD OBSTACLE.

13

Tournament Play

Try the Walter Hagen Philosophy

MOST CLUB GOLFERS PLAY LESS WELL IN TOURNAMENTS THAN THEY DO IN REGULAR GAMES WITH PALS.

EXTRA MENTAL AND PHYSICAL TENSION CREATED BY WANTING TO EXCEL IS GENERALLY THE CHIEF CAUSE.

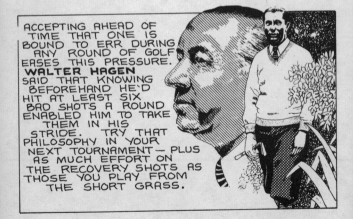

ACCEPTING AHEAD OF TIME THAT ONE IS BOUND TO ERR DURING ANY ROUND OF GOLF EASES THIS PRESSURE. **WALTER HAGEN** SAID THAT KNOWING BEFOREHAND HE'D HIT AT LEAST SIX BAD SHOTS A ROUND ENABLED HIM TO TAKE THEM IN HIS STRIDE. TRY THAT PHILOSOPHY IN YOUR NEXT TOURNAMENT — PLUS AS MUCH EFFORT ON THE RECOVERY SHOTS AS THOSE YOU PLAY FROM THE SHORT GRASS.

Put Safety First in Stroke-Play

BE REALISTIC, ESPECIALLY IN STROKE-PLAY WHERE THE RESULT DOESN'T DEPEND ON ANY ONE SHOT OR SINGLE HOLE.

BE SAFE RATHER THAN SORRY ANY TIME YOU'RE FACED WITH A TRULY RISKY SITUATION.

JM

FOR EXAMPLE, IF YOUR BALL IS IN A TIGHT LIE JUST SHORT OF A DEEP, WIDE TRAP WITH THE PIN TUCKED JUST BEYOND IT, THE PERCENTAGES IN TRYING TO GET CLOSE ARE DEFINITELY WAY AGAINST YOU.

DON'T COMPOUND THE ERROR: PLAY TO BE **ON THE GREEN SOMEWHERE**, EVEN IF THAT MEANS BEING LONG OR SHOOTING AWAY FROM THE HOLE.

Don't Forget to Hit the Ball

BEWARE BECOMING "TENTATIVE" AS THE COMPETITIVE SCREWS TIGHTEN. MANY MORE MATCHES ARE LOST THROUGH TRYING TO STEER THE BALL THAN BY OPENING THE SHOULDERS AND SWINGING FREELY.

MAKING MYSELF CONSCIOUSLY AWARE OF THE NEED TO ACTUALLY HIT THE BALL HAS HELPED ME A LOT AT SUCH TIMES.

I'LL CERTAINLY TRY FOR THE SMOOTHEST AND FULLEST SWING, OF COURSE, BUT THE THING I'LL TRY FOR MOST IS TO MAKE THAT SWING PRODUCE A HARD AND SOLID HIT THROUGH, RATHER THAN A FEARFUL JAB AT, THE BALL.

BECAUSE FEAR MAKES FOR HASTE, IT'S EASY TO "START DOWN BEFORE YOU'VE GONE BACK" ANY TIME YOU'RE UNDER PRESSURE OR FACING AN UNUSUALLY DIFFICULT SHOT.

"COMPLETE THE BACKSWING" IS MY FAVORITE THOUGHT AT SUCH TIMES.

CONSCIOUSLY CONCENTRATING ON SWINGING MY LEFT SHOULDER WELL UNDER MY CHIN, AND MY HANDS WELL ABOVE MY HEAD, ENSURES THAT I GO BACK BEFORE I TRY TO COME DOWN.

Win With Your Clubs Only

I HAVE NEVER KNOWINGLY USED "GAMESMAN-SHIP" AGAINST AN OPPONENT, BECAUSE I DON'T BELIEVE IT SHOULD PLAY A PART IN GOLF. SELF-RESPECT TO ME DEPENDS ON ACCOUNTING FOR MYSELF WITH MY CLUBS, NOT THROUGH SOME KIND OF PSYCHOLOGICAL WARFARE.

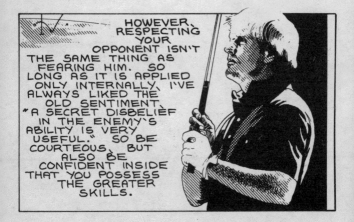

HOWEVER, RESPECTING YOUR OPPONENT ISN'T THE SAME THING AS FEARING HIM. SO LONG AS IT IS APPLIED ONLY INTERNALLY, I'VE ALWAYS LIKED THE OLD SENTIMENT, "A SECRET DISBELIEF IN THE ENEMY'S ABILITY IS VERY USEFUL." SO BE COURTEOUS, BUT ALSO BE CONFIDENT INSIDE THAT YOU POSSESS THE GREATER SKILLS.

Play the Course
Rather Than the Man

BASICALLY YOU'LL FARE BEST BY PLAYING THE COURSE RATHER THAN THE MAN IN MATCH-PLAY, SO CONCENTRATE CHIEFLY ON YOUR OWN GAME, NOT YOUR OPPONENT'S.

TIME TO PLAY THE MAN IS WHEN, HITTING FIRST, HE ENCOUNTERS SERIOUS TROUBLE LIKE OUT-OF-BOUNDS OR AN OBVIOUSLY UNPLAYABLE LIE.

WHEN THAT HAPPENS, DON'T TAKE ANY CHANCES.

SWALLOW YOUR PRIDE AND PLAY FOR A SURE WINNING SCORE, EVEN IF IT'S A BOGEY.

Don't Fear a "Better" Golfer

IN MATCH-PLAY, TRY NOT TO LET YOURSELF GET PSYCHED OUT BEFORE YOU BEGIN BY THE PROSPECT OF PLAYING A BETTER GOLFER. FORM ON THE DAY IS ALL THAT MATTERS, AND YOU WON'T KNOW HIS UNTIL PLAY BEGINS.

HE COULD BE "OFF" — JUST AS YOU COULD BE "ON."

GROSS 90
HANDICAP 18
NET 72

GROSS 84
HANDICAP 10
NET 74

BE SOCIABLE, BUT STRIVE TO PLAY YOUR OWN GAME AGAINST THE COURSE RATHER THAN AGAINST THE MAN. DON'T GAMBLE UNLESS AND UNTIL YOU ARE FORCED TO. MATCH-PLAY RECORDS SHOW THAT PAR GOLF GENERALLY WINS OVER THE LONG HAUL, SO PLAY FOR THAT FIRST — USING YOUR STROKES TO THAT END IF THE CONTEST INVOLVES HANDICAPS.

Never Coast in Match-Play

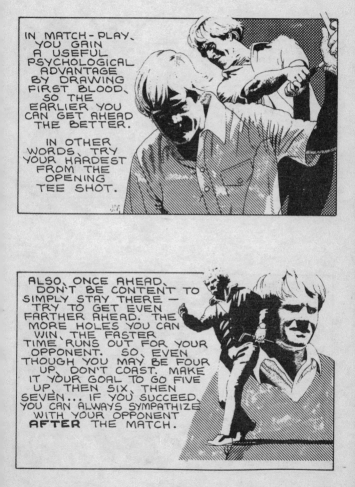

IN MATCH-PLAY, YOU GAIN A USEFUL PSYCHOLOGICAL ADVANTAGE BY DRAWING FIRST BLOOD, SO THE EARLIER YOU CAN GET AHEAD THE BETTER.

IN OTHER WORDS, TRY YOUR HARDEST FROM THE OPENING TEE SHOT.

ALSO, ONCE AHEAD, DON'T BE CONTENT TO SIMPLY STAY THERE — TRY TO GET EVEN FARTHER AHEAD. THE MORE HOLES YOU CAN WIN, THE FASTER TIME RUNS OUT FOR YOUR OPPONENT. SO, EVEN THOUGH YOU MAY BE FOUR UP, DON'T COAST. MAKE IT YOUR GOAL TO GO FIVE UP, THEN SIX, THEN SEVEN... IF YOU SUCCEED, YOU CAN ALWAYS SYMPATHIZE WITH YOUR OPPONENT **AFTER** THE MATCH.

Gamble Only When You Must

IN MATCH-PLAY, YOU MUST SOMETIMES GAMBLE HEAVILY IN RESPONSE TO YOUR OPPONENT'S PLAY.

FOR EXAMPLE, IF YOU'RE ONE DOWN WITH ONE TO PLAY AND HE'S ON THE GREEN, THEN YOU'VE GOT TO GO FOR IT, TOO, WHATEVER THE RISK.

WHEN THE GAME IS STROKE-PLAY, HOWEVER, KEEP IN MIND THE FACT THAT THE DECISION IS MADE OVER 18 HOLES, NEVER ON ANY ONE SHOT.

SO DON'T WRECK YOUR CHANCES BY TAKING NEEDLESS GAMBLES — PLAY THE PERCENTAGE SHOT OVER THE RISKY ONE AND STAY AWAY FROM DISASTERS.

BOGEY

Keep Cool—and Keep Trying

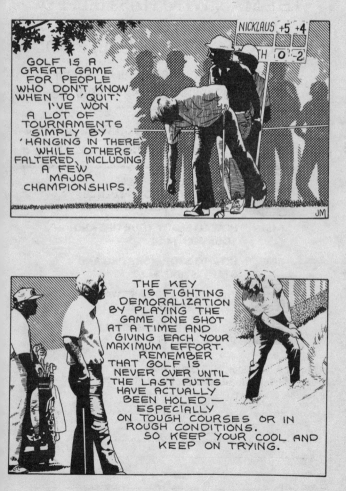

GOLF IS A GREAT GAME FOR PEOPLE WHO DON'T KNOW WHEN TO 'QUIT.' I'VE WON A LOT OF TOURNAMENTS SIMPLY BY 'HANGING IN THERE' WHILE OTHERS FALTERED, INCLUDING A FEW MAJOR CHAMPIONSHIPS.

THE KEY IS FIGHTING DEMORALIZATION BY PLAYING THE GAME ONE SHOT AT A TIME AND GIVING EACH YOUR MAXIMUM EFFORT. REMEMBER THAT GOLF IS NEVER OVER UNTIL THE LAST PUTTS HAVE ACTUALLY BEEN HOLED — ESPECIALLY ON TOUGH COURSES OR IN ROUGH CONDITIONS. SO KEEP YOUR COOL AND KEEP ON TRYING.